T0280162

PRAISE FOR RICH FETTKE AND
THE WISE INVESTOR

"Great stories have the power to change a person's views, their path, and their future and I believe this book will do just that and more. Rich has packed into this book all the knowledge and inspiration someone needs to build real wealth!"

BRANDON TURNER
Author of *The Book on Rental Property Investing*

"*The Wise Investor* is a wonderful read and will show you how to live a life you truly love. This book will dispel some of the myths of success you may have adopted along the way that have held you back from having what Rich Fettke so aptly points to as *real* wealth."

KRISTINE CARLSON
Co-author of the *Don't Sweat the Small Stuff* books

"In *The Wise Investor* Rich Fettke has created a story that will captivate you, educate you, and inspire you to behave in ways that put you on a path to financial freedom and a life of purpose."

ROBERT KIYOSAKI
Author of *Rich Dad Poor Dad*

"Rich and I have gotten to know each other well over the years and I can tell you from my personal experience that he 'lives and breathes' the deep, life-changing messages in this book. People chase money in a financial system that is not set up for you to win. There is a better way and it's not taught in schools, but it can be learned from watching others and in reading books like *The Wise Investor.*

One of the secrets we all chase is TIME and Rich does a masterful job of giving you some actionable steps you can take to wrestle back your life and reprioritize your daily habits. I highly recommend this book for anyone who has an open mind and wants to make some changes that will most certainly change their life."

KEN MCELROY
Author, entrepreneur and real estate investor

"Regardless of what stage you are at in your journey of investing for your freedom, *The Wise Investor* is a must read! You nailed it, Rich — I could not put it down. This book will inspire and challenge anyone to take action."

MIKE AYALA
Host of the *Investing for Freedom* podcast

"*The Wise Investor* is a powerful book filled with important and timely wisdom. Rich Fettke takes us on an inspiring journey and shows us how we can live with more freedom, joy, and abundance."

MIKE ROBBINS
Author of *We're All in This Together*

"*The Wise Investor* is a wise choice for anyone who wants to create financial freedom and an abundant life. Read this book to overcome your fear, move beyond your limiting beliefs, and take action to create YOUR dream and future. I'm giving it to my daughter (24) and son (22) — knowing it will give them the blueprint to create the income and freedom they want."

JON GORDON
Author of *The Carpenter* and *The Energy Bus*

THE WISE INVESTOR

INVESTOR

A MODERN PARABLE
ABOUT CREATING FINANCIAL FREEDOM
AND LIVING YOUR BEST LIFE

RICH FETTKE

HIGHLINE
PRESS

Published by:

Highline Press, an imprint of RDA Press LLC

Scottsdale, Arizona

Printed in Canada

First Edition Hardcase: 978-1-937832-73-5

realwealth.com

032022

FOREWORD

This is probably not the first book on finance you've ever picked up. People interested in their financial future tend to be serial readers of investment books. For some, this is because they have a growth mindset and constantly hunger for more knowledge and wisdom, no matter how much success they have already achieved. They know that there is always more to learn. For others, they just haven't realized the results they wanted. Were the books filled with one-size-fits-all formulas and useless information? Probably not. It is much more likely that the reason the books did not help is that the readers were not willing to do the work. Achieving financial freedom requires not only a shift in mindset but the commitment to learn about money... and apply what you learn.

When I wrote *Rich Dad Poor Dad* over twenty-five years ago, I shared the story of growing up with two dads. Both men were influential in my life, and their ideas about money could not have been more different. The rich have very different ideas about money than the poor and middle class. Wealthy people don't earn their money by working harder. They put their money to work for them by buying or building income-producing assets that bring passive income. I've talked with thousands of people around the world whose lives are different — and better — today because they've applied the lessons they've learned about putting their money to work.

The book you hold in your hands is not a how-to book on how to get rich, though it might inspire you to see wealth in a whole new way. It is not a how-to book on investing, though it might inspire you to learn more about investing. This is also not a how-to book on personal growth, goals, or self-discipline, though it might inspire you to take a hard look at yourself and how you work toward reaching your goals. The inspirational story told on these pages may shift the way you think about money, wealth, and time and show you new ways to create the life you want for yourself and your family.

Over the years I've noticed that there are lots of people who know what they need to do but for some reason refuse to do it. Financial success is not only about what you know, it's about how you behave. Rich Fettke has created a story that is more than just a fairy tale. It will captivate you, educate you, and inspire you to behave in ways that put you on a path to financial freedom and a life of purpose.

ROBERT KIYOSAKI

DEDICATION

This book is dedicated to the many mentors who have influenced my life. Especially my father, John Fettke, who showed me—by example—how to live with integrity, take responsibility, and to be the type of person that others can count on. I miss you and I love you, Papa.

A MESSAGE FROM THE AUTHOR

"Mr. Fettke," said my oncologist. I knew in my gut what he was going to say before he said it, but I hoped I was wrong. "The melanoma is not operable. I'm sorry, but best case—you probably have six months to live."

I was only thirty-seven. I had a beautiful wife, two wonderful daughters, a thriving coaching practice, and a freshly signed book deal with Simon & Schuster. I felt stoked and unstoppable. I had so many goals and dreams, but the doctor's words stopped me dead in my tracks and I spent the next several months in fear for my life, holding my breath with every new test conducted. It was a soul-searching moment in my life; full of tears, frustration, and despair.

Thankfully, the doctor's diagnosis was wrong; the melanoma didn't spread to my liver. That was twenty years ago, and every day since has seemed like a miracle that inspired me to make the most out of this life. Each day, I strive to be grateful for every second that I snatched back from the brink by spending time with the people I love and doing what brings me joy.

It's been said that every curse hides a blessing.

That initial diagnosis caused my wife to find a way to make ends meet if I died. She found mentors who helped guide her and led her to learn about real estate investing. After I was healed, we began to invest and learned a way to financial freedom. We wanted to help our friends and family do the same, so we formed what we thought would be a small group of people to learn about investing together. Today that small group has grown to over 60,000 members. The company that Kathy and I built, RealWealth, has helped thousands of people create financial freedom in their own lives.

Most people would probably expect someone like me to write a self-help book or a how-to book on investing. Instead, I wrote a story. Why? Because a story has the power to change perspectives, journeys, and futures. The power of a story goes beyond simply relaying facts and information; it emotionalizes information, allowing it to stimulate a change in both our attitudes and actions.

My hope is that this story inspires you first to get clarity about what your best life looks like and what really matters to you, and then to go and live it.

With that said, now is the best time in history for accessing information and learning, and I haven't helped tens of thousands of people achieve *real wealth* simply by telling them stories. At the end of this book, there are resources to help you assess what matters most to you in life, expand your financial intelligence, create more freedom with your time, and grow your wealth.

I wish you the best on your adventure.

CHAPTER ONE

Ryan's phone buzzed, and he looked up from his computer screen. He'd been cranking out code for the past three hours without a break, guzzling energy drinks and popping M&Ms, so the interruption provided a much-needed distraction. Rolling his shoulders a few times to work out the kinks, Ryan reached for his cell and swiped it open, expecting a message from his wife or maybe a member of his coding team.

Instead, a Facebook notification popped up. Apparently Billy, his college roommate, recently took a Disney vacation with his family. Pictures of a laughing woman and children looked back at Ryan through the phone screen. A smile flashed briefly across Ryan's face before a deep sense of longing washed it away. Tearing his gaze from the phone screen, Ryan looked instead at the collage of photos taped above his office phone: he and his roommate in their cap and gowns after graduation, some of his kids growing up through the years.

Finally, his eyes landed on one of Karisa and him on their honeymoon in Hawaii, hugging each other in front of an azure ocean. They'd been so filled with excitement back then, making plans and planning dreams. Next to the photo hung an index card with his favorite quote from college: 'The more that you read, the more things you will know. The more that you learn, the more places you'll go'—Dr. Seuss.

That was their dream back then—going places. Traveling the world. Now, twelve years later, he was forced to admit that they hadn't gone anywhere. Rubbing the back of his neck, he looked at the financial books lined up in a row on his desk: Dave Ramsey, David Bach, Robert Kiyosaki. He remembered diligently reading them during his lunch breaks when he began his job, trying to figure out the secret to making money. He flipped through one now, *Rich Dad Poor Dad* smiling at the neat notes in the margins, then returned it. What had he done with all that knowledge? Nothing. Were they any closer to their dreams? Not really.

While Billy was taking his family on exciting vacations, Ryan had worked his way up to be a coding team leader, getting raises along the way, but it had never been enough for the kind of life they wanted to live. The books he'd read all agreed that investing and earning some passive income was key, but having enough money to invest was the problem. It seemed like making a little over six figures and maxing his 401(k) should put them in good shape for that sort of thing, but once all their expenses were covered, there wasn't enough cash left over for investing. They'd save, then along came the kids, then save some more, and bam—a car wreck out of nowhere or some other random expense. There was always something. The books never seemed to address those life-gets-in-the-way things. No matter how much more he made, their expenses seemed to keep pace, and they never seemed to get ahead. Ryan touched the quote. *I know a lot, Dr. Seuss,* he thought to himself. *Enough to know that I don't know enough.*

Maybe it was time to read the books again. Even if travel was a pipe dream, he really needed to start thinking about the future, saving for the kids' college and his own retirement. He needed to stop procrastinating.

His cell rang.

"Hey, babe," he said.

"Are you on your way?"

"Huh?"

"Did you forget that we have to pick up the car at the shop this afternoon? They close at five," said Karisa.

Oh, damn. "Sorry, I did forget. Can you get someone else to help you? I'm a little behind at work right now."

"No, I can't. You said you'd be home."

He bit on the end of his already well-chewed pen. "Okay, I'll tell Howard I need to leave early. Hopefully, it won't be a big problem." Howard wasn't going to like that. They had a deadline coming up.

"Really? You've been working late every day this week. The least they could do is let you go a couple of hours early. Also, the insurance deductible is $1,000. We'll need to pay when we pick up the car."

Ryan's stomach clenched. "Jeez!"

"The total was over $3,000."

"Okay, I'm heading home now." Ryan ran his hand through his hair.

"Please don't be late. I need the car tomorrow. We need groceries, and I have to take the kids to their sports practices."

"I'll be there."

He hung up and debated which credit card to use for the deductible. They had savings, but that was supposed to be their emergency fund. They had both agreed they wouldn't touch that. But did the interest on the credit card outweigh using the savings?

The clock on his computer said 3:34. He needed to leave now if he wanted to miss the traffic. Sighing audibly, he grabbed his coat and backpack and headed for his boss's office.

Howard looked up through the open door as he approached. "Ryan, get in here."

"Hey, Howard. I need to leave early to pick up my wife's car at the shop."

"Sit down. We need to talk," said Howard.

"But I really—"

"Sit down, Ryan."

The brown leather chair creaked as Ryan sat down. At fifty-seven, Howard looked every bit the middle manager with his graying hair and paunch. They'd always gotten along well, and Howard had even given him his last raise.

The analytics manager steepled his hands. "Ryan, I like you. You're a hard worker, dependable, and smart. Reminds me of myself at your age."

There was a pause, and Ryan almost said 'thanks,' but Howard pushed on.

"You're on your way up, but you need to focus. We have a management position opening soon. One of the Junior Operations managers is leaving in the summer, and you would be perfect for that job, running herd over the other coders. You're already one of our best and have done all the training."

"I don't know what to say."

"Well, are you interested? Are you willing to do the work?"

Ryan nodded. "I am. What do I have to do?"

"I thought I had you pegged right. I'll be honest with you, it will mean longer hours in the office, coming in on the weekends. You have to do the time. Also, upper management likes to see their managers giving back to the community."

Ryan frowned. "Like donating?"

"Donating is good of course, but they like to see you getting your hands dirty, representing the company at charitable functions—like the Habitat for Humanity Team Building event tomorrow."

Ryan shook his head. "I don't know anything about building a house."

Howard wrote on a notepad and tore out the page, handing it to Ryan. "You don't have to know anything. They will either teach you or give you a job that doesn't require any skills. Look, the entire leadership team is participating. Call this number and they'll tell you when and where to be. Make sure to wear a company shirt."

"Okay, but I was going to work on the Liza Project this weekend."

"I guess you'll have to come in on Sunday to finish that up. You and your team work it out."

Ryan groaned silently. He never seemed to have enough time in his life.

"And you should find yourself a mentor."

Ryan looked up. "A mentor?"

"A business mentor, someone you can go to when you need advice, who can guide you through the management hurdles."

"So, can you be my mentor?"

Howard laughed. "You don't want me as a mentor." He stood. "Find yourself a mentor who can make an impact on your life. There will be a number of senior management at the Habitat event, you should definitely talk to them."

Ryan stood, a little confused. He wasn't sure exactly what a mentor would do for him. He had been fine so far without one.

Howard thrust his hand out, and Ryan shook it. "I know you have what it takes, Ryan. Put in the extra hours at work, spend some time at that charity thing, find a mentor, and I'm sure you'll be the right man for the job. The position will open in a few months, so focus and keep your nose to the grindstone."

"Okay, you can count on me."

Ryan thought about everything Howard had told him on the drive home. Putting in more time at the office wasn't going to make Karisa happy, but the raise could help them get ahead of their expenses and finally start investing in their future. He patted the real estate investing book he had selected from his desk library.

"Call Karisa," he said out loud.

She picked up after two rings. "Hey hun, you almost here?" she asked.

"Yeah, in about fifteen minutes. Hey, Howard kind of offered me a promotion today."

"That's fantastic!" she said. "You really deserve it."

Ryan paused. "But he said I'm going to have to work more at the office, and that I have to do some charity work this weekend."

She was quiet for a moment. "Michael has a soccer game on Saturday."

"I know he does, babe, but this promotion could mean a big raise. We could use that, maybe finally get us on track."

He heard her sigh.

"It's just..." She paused again. "It's just that you're working such long hours already. You hardly ever spend time with the kids. They aren't getting any younger, you know."

"I know, but this promotion would be a good thing. If we just stick with it, we can get there. I'll be home in a bit. We can talk on the way to pick up the car."

"Okay, I guess. See you at home." She hung up.

Despite Karisa's obvious frustration, Ryan felt excited. She would understand once she realized how much the promotion would benefit their family. He smiled.

He'd get that promotion, become an investing expert, and then—*The more places you'll go!*

Learn about investing, check. Working extra hours, check. Charity work tomorrow, check. Now, to find a mentor.

CHAPTER
TWO

"Ow!" Ryan shook his thumb for what seemed like the hundredth time; it was beginning to turn purple.

What was it the project manager had said this morning—to take pride in the blood, sweat, and tears they would pour into this building today? *He had that right*, Ryan thought as he inspected the damage. *No blood yet, but swelling for sure.*

Ryan wasn't particularly skilled in construction. He owned some tools for odd jobs around the house—somewhere. Maybe in the garage? Still, the last four hours had passed pretty quickly as he mindlessly hammered away, and the blister forming on his hand had begun to throb in time with his pulse. The work was almost therapeutic in a way though, all the physical exertion while his mind drifted.

He thought about the promotion. It would solve so many of his problems: pay off the credit cards, start putting some money away for the kids' college funds, and finally, they could start investing in their future, which was coming up way too fast. They could finally get ahead of the rat race; finally breathe.

He needed to impress Howard and the leadership team.

Speaking of the leadership team.

Ryan stood and stretched, basking in the sun that peeked through the clouds while looking around in amazement at all that he and the other volunteers had accomplished in such a short period of time. CaptivSoft had signed up for one of Habitat for Humanity's Team Building volunteer projects, and Ryan recognized a lot of senior managers present, spread out around the half-built house. This house was one of four that the nonprofit was orchestrating this week. Ryan hadn't been a big believer on arrival, and he still wasn't sure about all the details, but even one house in a week would have impressed him, let alone four.

He didn't see Howard anywhere. The Sales and Operations managers talked near the home's entrance, apparently on some kind of self-imposed break. He'd heard good things about them, though never had any interaction. The senior leaders weren't much for mingling. He just needed to figure out his approach.

"How are we doing here?"

John Weise knelt on one knee, admiring Ryan's work. He wasn't the site manager, but he seemed to be the de facto chief for building the frame. A fit man, he looked to be in his early fifties and seemed to know his way around the project, appearing at random moments, checking in, and making small corrections to the volunteers' techniques.

"Wow, okay Ryan, you've made some good progress here." He grabbed a few nails out of his vest and positioned one into a spot Ryan had already finished. "Just some reinforcement," he continued. "Try and get the nails center of this junction, about there." The nail went in with two precise blows, exactly centered between Ryan's three crooked nails.

Ryan had to admit, he was a tad jealous. "So, do you spend every night fixing all the volunteers' mistakes?" asked Ryan, admiring the perfectly placed nail.

John laughed, a deep but pleasant sound. "Naw, it's all good."

"Mr. Weise." A teenage girl appeared.

"I told you, Bridgette, it's just 'John'." He turned and gave her his full attention. "What's up?"

"John, yeah, so hypothetically, if I put in a window upside down, how would I fix that?"

He chuckled. "You're in the back of the house, right?"

She nodded, her ponytail bouncing.

"Okay, I'll be back there in a minute to show you."

She smiled brightly and scampered away.

"I think you're lying about your nocturnal activities."

John shook his head. "There's nothing that can't be fixed with a little elbow grease, and no one learns without breaking a few boards first." He stood up. "You do good work, Ryan. Thanks for coming out today."

The compliment left Ryan speechless for a second. "No problem, John."

John smiled. "We'll talk later."

Ryan watched him leave, following in Bridgette's footsteps.

Their lunch break came soon after. Ryan had intended on speaking with some of the CaptivSoft managers, but they all clustered on the front lawn in cliques, like high schoolers, and he didn't see a good way to insert himself. He seemed to be the only one there from the company that wasn't in management. Ryan finally caught sight of Howard sitting with one group.

Ryan racked his brain. Maybe he could pair up with one of the managers on a project this afternoon, one that Howard was working on too, and his boss could make some introductions. They could all hammer some nails together and make connections. But who would finish his project? He couldn't just quit the task he'd been assigned. For some reason, he felt he'd be letting John down. Ryan looked around and saw the man himself eating lunch alone on the half-built front porch. Should he ask? Would John think less of him?

Ryan didn't see much choice. If he didn't connect with any of the, he'd basically missed Michael's soccer game and wasted a day for nothing.

John looked up as Ryan approached. "Have a seat. Got any lunch?"

Ryan shook his head. "I was a late addition, and I didn't get the memo about bringing your own lunch. All I have is some leftover donuts from breakfast."

"That's a shame, mostly for your health though. I got some extra here."

Ryan held up his hands. "I couldn't, really, thanks."

"Don't be ridiculous, I always pack extra. This isn't my first rodeo. There's always someone at the site without." He pushed a lettuce wrap with sprouts and tomatoes hanging out the end into Ryan's hand. It didn't exactly look like the sort of thing he would normally eat, but it certainly looked better than going hungry. "I insist. You have to keep up your strength. I have more work for you this afternoon."

Ryan winced at the work comment. "You really seem to know what you're doing around here. Do you work in construction or something?" Ryan settled down next to John and started in on the wrap while he waited for a reply.

John chuckled warmly at the question. "No, nothing like that. I just do enough of these Habitat events to know my way around a hammer. Is this your first event?"

Ryan wrinkled his nose. "Is it that obvious?" he answered with an easy grin and a shrug. "Honestly, I didn't even know about this thing until yesterday. I'm up for a promotion at work, and my boss told me that coming to this event could be a good way to get noticed by the leadership team and would help me find a mentor. Speaking of which, do you mind if I move on to another part of the house? I need to schmooze with the big guys before the day is done."

"You have to schmooze to find a mentor?" John asked.

Ryan shrugged. "Do you have a better idea?"

"I don't know buddy, it seems like a real mentor would seek you out because he sees your potential and wants to share knowledge to help you level up. I wouldn't think needing to be schmoozed is a sign of a good leader."

Ryan thought about that for a second. To be honest, that made a lot of sense.

"Mr. Weise, I mean, John."

Bridgette had snuck up behind them.

"Yes," said John, standing up to face her.

"Hypothetically..."

"I'll be there in a minute."

"Okay," she said, energetically retreating into the house.

John turned to Ryan. "Hey, if you need to schmooze, knock yourself out, I'll find someone else to finish up. On another note though, you should come back on Friday afternoon. We'll have the house finished and the inspections done this week, then we'll turn over the keys. It's a really special moment for the owners. And we'll have a little celebration event afterward."

"I'll think about it John, thanks. I have some things to do, but I'll look at my calendar."

"Okay, let me know." John turned to head back into the house.

Ryan stood. "Hey, John, seriously though, you might want to consider firing some of your free help. Bridgette can't be worth the trouble."

"Who else would volunteer if I did that?" John said over his shoulder. "Anyway, she's the daughter of the new owner. I can't fire her. She lives here."

Ryan spent the afternoon mingling with the managers, who mostly spoke about themselves and their accomplishments. Not once did they ask about Ryan or what he did for the company. At the end of the afternoon, Ryan hadn't engaged any of them for mentorship. And John's words were echoing in the back of his mind. *A real mentor should see your potential and want to help you level up.* He just didn't feel like any of these men would be the mentor he needed.

Truth be told, Ryan didn't know what to look for in a mentor. He'd never even considered it until his conversation with Howard. What did Ryan want? Someone who believed in him. Someone who could make him better. Someone who had something to teach him.

Ryan thought about his career at CaptivSoft. He had gotten to the level of team leader by his own initiative, no one had mentored him or held his hand. He was proud of that, to be sure, but after that short conversation with John, disappointment began to creep in. Everyone in the company seemed to be focused on themselves. What did

Ryan want? More pay in order to fund his dreams. Would climbing the corporate ladder give him that? If so, how did reading all those investment books factor in? It would have been nice if someone in the company had stepped forward to help and teach him.

Ryan said his goodbyes to the CaptivSoft managers, watching them drive away, then turned to go to his own car when John approached him with a couple of bottled waters.

"In a hurry?" John asked.

"I can stay for a bit, I guess."

"How did the schmoozing go?"

Ryan smiled. "Not great, I might not be cut out for that sort of thing."

John shrugged. "There's worse things to be bad at, I guess."

Ryan nodded at the house. "So, we're done?"

"Close. They'll finish up the details tomorrow morning and then have the inspectors check it. Thanks for the help today."

"My pleasure. So, Habitat doesn't pay you? You just run these events for free?"

John took another swallow of water. "I like to give back, you know. I've just spent a lot of time volunteering for

Habitat over the years, so when they need help they ask me to manage events every now and then. For my day job, I own a gym down the road, and I'm also a real estate investor."

"Aha, that's why you're so fit."

"Among other reasons. I like a lot of outdoor sports, and this area is great for that," John said, as he put his trash in a backpack at his feet.

"My wife, Karisa, and I used to do a lot of hiking and camping back in the day. Now that the kids are getting older, maybe we should get out there again."

"Well, I can definitely recommend some places."

Ryan nodded. "I may take you up on that. And you invest in real estate? I've been thinking about getting into that, too."

"I love it. I think it's one of the best ways to make money in this modern world."

Ryan felt even more determined to reread the book he'd brought home.

"So, how old are your kids?" John asked.

"Michael is eleven and Joy is eight." Ryan thought about the soccer game he had already missed. "In fact, I need to get back."

"No worries. Hey, seriously, come by next Friday around six for the Key Ceremony, and bring the family."

"You really don't take no for an answer, do you."

"Not usually."

CHAPTER
THREE

"Dad, are you listening to me?"

Ryan's eyes were on his computer. "Yeah, the basketball hoop is broken."

"No, I said we haven't played hoops in a while."

Ryan looked up. "Oh." His son stood in his office doorway with a basketball in his hand, and Ryan had no idea how long he'd been there. "I—" Ryan's phone vibrated and Howard's name appeared. "Just let me take this call, and I—"

"Never mind," Michael muttered as he disappeared into the house.

Ryan took a breath. That went poorly. "Good evening, Howard," Ryan answered.

"Hey, Ryan, the clients called. They have to move the meeting to tomorrow afternoon. We'll start at 4 pm sharp, so it will probably be a long day. Any problems with that?"

Ryan let out a slow breath. "No problem at all."

And he meant it.

His team had bailed on him at the office today, forcing Ryan to stay late and finalize everything himself. Irritated over the whole situation, Ryan contemplated telling Howard. The software required some additional debugging, and Ryan had ended up making a whole new subroutine. He was still a little behind and having tomorrow morning to tweak and review everything felt like a huge bonus.

"You ready?" asked Howard.

"Don't worry, we got this."

"Good. I'm glad I made you lead on this. I knew I could count on you. Oh yeah, did you enjoy the charity thing yesterday?"

"It was great, really great. Thanks for doing the introductions. I spent the afternoon working with some of the management team. They seemed nice."

"No problem, those guys are solid. It's good that you're on their radar. Now they know who you are."

"Nothing like hammering nails to bring people together."

"Got that right. Alright, see you tomorrow. Let's show those guys at Liza Inc. that we're the right company to partner with them."

"Will do. See you tomorrow."

After the call, Ryan thought about the Habitat for Humanity work he'd done yesterday. It had felt really good putting in the hours to help Bridgette and her family, and he thought he'd even gotten better at hammering nails by the end; that's what John said anyway.

"Dinner's ready," Karisa interrupted his thoughts.

Her short, clipped tone left no room for doubt—Ryan was still in the dog house. He'd called her from the office today, telling her he had to work through the afternoon to get ready for the meeting, and that he would miss Joy's performance. Again. She had answered coolly as if she had expected it. Surely, she knew this was for the best. She had to understand that his efforts benefited both of them, the whole family. It would all be worth it after he got the promotion.

He finished his Red Bull, closed his laptop, and went to the dining room.

The kids were already at the table.

"I sold two more of my wall art projects today," Karisa told him once she'd finally managed to settle down at her own place.

"Mmm, huh," Ryan said, chewing his food. His phone dinged and he continued chewing as he swiped through the message. One of the team members asking when the meeting was tomorrow.

"Why does dad get to have his phone at the table?" asked Michael with his mouth full.

"He doesn't," said Karisa. "Do you, Ryan?"

Ryan looked up. Her tone had changed. She was serious, and he put the phone face down on the table.

"Of course not. Sorry. It's just, this contract tomorrow is a big deal, and I really want to impress…" He stopped and shrugged his shoulders. "Anyway, what were you saying about your wall art?" He took another bite, giving her his full attention.

"I sold two."

Ryan's phone dinged. He glanced at Karisa and reached down to turn it off.

Karisa smiled slightly.

He swallowed. "That's really great, babe. Congratulations. How many is that so far?"

"Twenty-eight. I think that's pretty good for two months. There could be a really good market for them, I just need to find it."

Ryan nodded his head. "Sure there is." He took another bite. He still had a lot to do tonight—make sure the team was prepared with the updates, review the slides again, debug the software and check the coding.

He swallowed again. "Have you looked into using Etsy? I hear that's a good platform."

Silence. Ryan looked up.

"I'm selling on Etsy. What do you think I'm talking about?"

Shoot. "Yeah, but I mean, are you using their guidelines? Are you charging enough to cover all the materials and postage? And your time, don't forget you need to pay yourself back for your time."

She paused. "I think so. I left that document with all my expenses on your desk like you asked. Did you look at it?"

"Ah, babe, I'm sorry. I'll look at it right after dinner, I promise."

"I'm just starting out, and I'm sure the process will get faster, so maybe I'm not charging a premium rate for my time yet."

"Can I be excused?" Joy asked.

Karisa looked at her clean plate. "Of course, honey. Did you finish your homework?"

Joy nodded. "We didn't have much because tomorrow is career day." She hopped off the chair and ran to her room.

Oh no, thought Ryan, *Career Day*.

Karisa stared at him. "You forgot, didn't you."

"No."

She nodded, apparently relieved. "So, tomorrow afternoon—what? Why are you shaking your head?"

Ryan wiped his mouth. His gut clenched. He already knew how this would end, and it felt like he was barreling down a steep hill with no breaks. "So, I didn't forget, just to be clear, but Howard called right before dinner. The client changed the meeting time to tomorrow afternoon."

"So, call him back and tell him you can't make it. Tell them to have someone else give the presentation."

Ryan started to think through who else on his team could give the presentation, but he was team lead on the project. Passing off the responsibility to someone else would just make him look weak. It definitely wouldn't help him get the promotion.

"Babe, this isn't a good time. They're depending on me to explain the software that I helped create."

"I thought you had other team members working with you on this."

Ryan shook his head. "I'm the lead coder, and I made some changes today without the team. Anyway, I promised Howard I'd lead the meeting."

"And you promised your daughter you'd attend Career Day."

He sighed. "I can't do it, Karisa, there's just no way."

She stared at him icily, and he looked down at his plate, moving food around with his fork.

When he looked up, he was alone.

———————

Ryan cleared the table and went back to his office.

He couldn't concentrate fully though. The silent treatment was becoming a more common solution to their problems than he wanted to admit.

Ryan started going through the mail, separating the bills and the junk. A postcard caught his eye.

FREE SEMINAR!!
MAKE MONEY THROUGH
REAL ESTATE FLIPS

Looking for ways to generate extra income but aren't sure how?

If you are motivated to make money through 'Real Estate Flips' but lack the knowledge and resources, attend our FREE Millionaire Maker Seminar! With over 30 years of experience and millions of dollars in sales, we have the pulse on the best ways to generate a profit using our innovative system in identifying estate sales and distressed owners wanting to sell their homes in prime real estate locations.

- Learn about the different kinds of property flips that can make you rich overnight

- Hear about how our clients use our innovative techniques to make big profits

- Meet our panel of experts

The back of the card had the dates and address and a webpage where he could register. It would take place this coming Wednesday evening.

Ryan put his hand on the real estate book he'd brought home.

He smelled Karisa's essential oils right before she put her hands on his shoulders.

Ryan turned. "I'm sorry, babe, really. Once I finish with this client tomorrow, I'll be more present, I promise." He hugged her, still sitting, ear against her stomach.

"You've been so busy lately," she said. "We've barely seen you all weekend."

"I know." He looked up at her. "I made a friend at the Habitat for Humanity thing. He invited us to a BBQ or something, next Friday. We should go."

"I don't know."

"It'll be fun, and he invited the kids too. The whole family, together for once."

She was silent for a bit, and it felt good just to hold her.

"I'm pregnant."

He froze. Doubts, responsibility, fear—he felt it all, the invisible weight crushing him.

"Aren't you happy?"

Then he relaxed. He breathed deeply, lifted her shirt enough to kiss her belly, then looked up into the eyes of the woman he loved more than anything.

"I couldn't be happier." He stood and wrapped his arms around her.

Even the money from the promotion wouldn't help them catch up once the baby came. They needed a change. Maybe it was time to listen to some experts. He wasn't one hundred percent sure the real estate seminar from the flyer was going to change his life, but he needed to start taking action for their future. As Karisa left the room, Ryan opened the browser on his computer and clicked the register button.

CHAPTER
FOUR

R yan paused in front of the frosted glass door, staring anxiously at the brass plated sign mounted at eye level with the name Dave Patterson, Vice President of Operations, printed in neatly stenciled lettering. Patterson had a reputation for having a temper, but Ryan had never had any interaction with him before. The administrative assistant hadn't given him much information, and he wondered what this meeting was all about.

He knocked on the half-open door.

"Come on in, Ryan."

If Dave hadn't been so tall, he would have been fat. As it was, the man was huge. When he stood up, he towered over Ryan's five foot nine frame by another half foot, and was probably that much broader, too.

"Have a seat, please," Dave offered after shaking Ryan's extended hand. "Howard has told me great things about you, and I hear we have you to thank for the success of the Liza Inc Project."

"Thanks, sir, we all do our part for the company."

"That's the right attitude. I have to tell you, your name has been dropped for a Junior Management position coming up, and I think you really are what we're looking for."

"I appreciate that, sir."

"I just want to make sure you are mentally prepared for it. It's a lot of responsibility to manage multiple projects simultaneously. We work long hours to get things done, but the rewards are worth it."

Ryan's stomach tightened. More hours. He knew that of course, it wasn't the first time he had heard it from others in the company. Anxiety curled in his gut at the idea of working more, especially with Karisa being pregnant, but what could he do?

"I understand what you're saying, sir. I've worked hard for the contracts, I have a proven track record in the company."

Dave nodded. "Yes you do, Ryan."

Something bugged Ryan, a stray thought he couldn't get out of his mind, and before he could stop himself, it just came out. "Sir, can I ask you a somewhat personal question?"

Dave paused, surprise evident on his face. "Why sure. What is it?"

"You've worked for CaptivSoft for how long, over thirty years?"

"Thirty-six, next month."

"Thirty-six years. That's a long time. And do you have any regrets? What I mean is, would you have done anything differently?"

Dave pursed his lips thoughtfully. "You know, Ryan, I started at this company as a coder, before it was even a profession. And I busted my ass to get where I am today. Now, I live in a huge house, drive an expensive car, and take a two-week ski vacation to Switzerland every year. It really is worth it to keep busting your ass if that's what you're asking."

"And your family? Did they adapt to your work schedule?"

Dave laughed. "Well, not my first wife. She couldn't appreciate what I was trying to build for us. Families adjust, or you adjust to a new family. That seems to be the trend in the leadership team around here."

"Thanks for the advice, sir."

"You're welcome. Keep up the good work."

On his way back to his desk, Ryan considered what Dave had said. He didn't want Karisa to have to adapt. Going to the real estate seminar tonight meant forging a different path for his family.

He took the elevator down.

He didn't want to have to work overtime in ten years. He didn't want to keep missing soccer games, first steps and first words. Maybe this seminar wouldn't change his life, but he'd never know unless he tried. He needed to start taking action.

———————————

"How many of you want to learn how to make some money?"

Enthusiastic cheering followed the speaker's question, and the conference room filled with raised hands.

"How many of you don't know why you're here and came because a friend dragged you here?"

Laughter and a few hands.

"Well, whatever the reason, we're glad you came. Welcome to Roy Clark's Prosperity Through Property Program. I'm going to be upfront here, this seminar only covers the bare bones of making money through real estate. We're only here for two hours, there's no way to get through all the information in that amount of time. This will just get you a taste of Mr. Clark's three-day Level Up Mentorship program this weekend. If that isn't what you were expecting, I'm sorry, and feel free to leave now." No one moved.

The speaker continued to talk about the program, but Ryan already knew most of the details. He had Googled this particular seminar and watched some YouTube videos made by people who had actually attended. He knew it was a sales pitch for the longer course, but that made sense to him. It was inconceivable that he would learn anything beyond what he had read in his real estate investment books in two hours.

"Online, the three-day Level Up Mentorship program would cost you $10,000, but because you guys have invested your time at this seminar, we know you are motivated. So, we're offering you a fifty percent discount, but only if you sign up today. At the back of the room, we have our staff ready to help you sign up. And as an added bonus, we'll give you an additional ticket to bring your spouse or another friend. And remember, this is one hundred percent refundable, and the venue has limited seating, so don't miss out."

A few people got up, excusing themselves through the rows, and went to the back of the room. Still not totally convinced, Ryan decided to wait and hear more. The speaker brought up some slides, telling his audience that real estate offered one of the most secure ways to make money in this time of market chaos. He discussed a lot of topics that Ryan already knew about—wholesaling, rental properties, and flips. He mentioned some other programs that Roy Clark offered which were separate from the real estate programs, but Ryan tuned them out. Real estate was the way forward for him.

"We get deeper into the process over the weekend course where we talk about Roy's three-step system." The speaker began ticking off his fingers. "*Finding* the right property, *financing* your deal, and *finalizing* the process."

So far, Ryan didn't see anything wrong with the brief. He wasn't an expert, but the information matched what he already knew. And it wasn't a whole lot of money to invest in his future.

"If this process works," asked an audience member, "why are you and Roy Clark here? What's in it for you?"

The speaker smiled. "That's an excellent question. Roy is out there doing what he does best, implementing and honing his process. He wants to give these seminars because he wants to share this knowledge. You all know his story and where he came from. He had to learn these lessons the hard way and he doesn't think it has to be that way. We give these seminars in order to find that small, motivated group of individuals that wants to take control of their finances and their life and be a part of Roy's team. Let me ask you a question." The speaker walked out into the middle of the conference room with his mic. "Tell me, if there was something you could do to make more money and get rich, would you do it?"

Heads nodded, and some even said yes.

"Being rich isn't something to be ashamed of. No one should be afraid to live their best life. Can you imagine what you would do if you had enough money to live the life of your dreams?"

More nods and half the crowd said yes.

"Roy Clark has helped thousands of people just like you, with his millionaire secrets that help you stop acting like the poor and start living like the rich. Are you interested in learning those secrets?"

"Yes." Ryan found himself replying now too. He saw some of the people who had gone to the back of the room returning to their seats with large yellow bags.

"What about all the bad press this course has gotten lately?" someone asked.

The speaker returned to the front of the room.

"Look, there's always going to be those who aren't happy, no matter what you give them. This program isn't magic, you have to do the work. If you aren't willing to do the work then, I have to tell you, not much is going to change in your life. But if you follow the steps in the three-day course, and you show up willing to give the effort, you will reap what you sow. In order to have what other people don't have, you have to be willing to do what others won't do." He pointed at the person who asked the question. "Look, if you don't think this program is right for you, then you're probably right, and you shouldn't sign up. Leave that space for someone who is willing to do the work."

Ryan's hands hovered over his phone. He began composing a message to Karisa but stopped halfway. He was going to explain the opportunity and how much it cost, but he realized she would never agree. Karisa liked to play it safe, but that wouldn't get them where they wanted to be. He looked up at the speaker. *Leave that space for someone who is willing to do the work.* It was time to make a difference in their financial life. Karisa probably wouldn't agree to investing in this opportunity, but once she saw the payoff, she'd be fine with it.

"We have ten spots left, folks," said the speaker after a man in a suit whispered something into his ear.

Ryan stood up. He was willing to do the work. This was what he had been looking for.

Ryan arrived home and saw Karisa's car in the driveway.

He had emptied a good chunk of their emergency fund to pay for the weekend course. $5,000. Now he needed to tell Karisa. They had agreed to make decisions together on spending anything over $500. He should have asked before he spent it. He should have told her about the seminar. He should have done a lot of things.

Still, Roy Clark himself would be there. They guaranteed a house flip in the first month. If that was true, Karisa would never even know until after he made money back.

He felt horrible. He felt sick. He needed to tell her.

An unusual quiet greeted him.

He opened the door in the kitchen that led to the garage.

Karisa worked with her back to him, bent over a wooden table that was too short for the chair she sat in. Scattered around her were frames, plants, and different-sized moss art configurations. At the end of the table was a completed project. Thin wood framed a collage of different shades of green moss arranged around branches and leaves. Music blared from her phone, old nineties rock.

He remembered Dave's words. *Families adjust, or you adjust to a new family.* The whole reason he decided to do this course was to provide for his family, plan for the future, and be around more. Now, his lies might destroy what he was trying to save. He had to tell her.

He watched her move to the beat of a Bon Jovi song as she worked, and couldn't help but smile.

Coming up behind her, he hugged her, and she jumped.

"Oh, it's you." She turned and smiled too.

"Expecting someone else?"

"You never know."

He gave her a peck on the lips. "I'm going to try and come home earlier from now on."

"That would be nice, but I won't hold my breath."

"Where are the kids?"

"I think they're in their rooms playing video games. Homework is all done. Believe it or not, this is what the house sounds like every night when you're not here."

"Noted." Ryan looked down and realized he hadn't been in the garage in a long time, not since she took it over as her workshop. "Show me," he said, gesturing at the materials spread out before her.

Karisa spent the next hour walking him through the process of making her moss wall art. She showed him the orders she had lined up and the Word document she used to keep track of everything.

"I could probably make something, even a simple spreadsheet, that would make the accounting easier," Ryan told her.

"That would be wonderful, hun."

She turned off her desk light, and they walked back into the house with their arms around each other.

"Have you gained some weight?" she asked, squeezing his side.

"Let's not go there. There's never enough time for the gym."

Karisa removed food from the fridge.

"Did you decide if you want to go to the Habitat for Humanity thing on Friday?"

She spooned lasagna onto a plate and put it into the microwave. "I guess. It would be good to get out of the house as a family."

Ryan hugged her from behind.

"What's got into you?"

Man, I love this woman, thought Ryan. *I have to tell her.* "I can't hug my wife?"

"Did something happen at work?" she asked.

"No, work was good. I spoke to Dave Patterson today. He seemed to think I was a sure thing for the promotion."

"Oh my gosh, that's great!" She hugged him. "That's so amazing, I'm so proud of you."

She separated from him and looked into his face. "What's wrong? I thought you wanted this promotion."

He nodded slowly. "I do, it's just…"

He hugged her again, tight. He couldn't tell her. He couldn't bear to see the disappointment. He'd tell her after he made the money back.

"What is it?" she asked quietly into his ear.

He held her hands and stared at her for a moment. "If I get the promotion, I'll be working longer hours."

She smiled. "I know, but not forever."

No, not forever, he thought.

CHAPTER FIVE

"I thought you told me it was a gym," said Karisa, as they pulled into the parking lot.

The warehouse-sized building rose before them. A giant wall of windows revealed people in different stages of climbing the indoor rock walls, hanging from ropes, and leaping between ledges. Above the double entry doors hung a large, dark-green sign, its yellow lettering declaring it to be 'The Adventure Gym.'

Smaller lettering underneath read, 'Fun for Any Age.'

"He always called it a gym. It must be one of those climbing places," said Ryan.

"Cool!" said Michael from the back.

"I don't think I should be doing this given my current situation," said Karisa.

Ryan put his hand on her stomach. "Look, Risa, we'll just stay for a bit, say 'hi', and go home."

She smiled and nodded. "Okay."

A fit woman in her late forties came out of the front doors and walked straight up to Karisa, wrapping her in a hug. "I'm Jill, John's wife. We saw you at the Habitat key ceremony, but I didn't get a chance to introduce myself. And who are these guys?" she asked, gesturing to the children.

"That's Michael," Karisa answered, then looked down at her daughter and placed her hand on her head. "And this is Joy."

"We have some activities set up for the kids. I'll show you where." Jill led the way, talking excitedly to Karisa as they all followed her into the building.

Inside was controlled chaos.

The ceiling must have been eight stories tall, and in every direction there were people running, jumping, climbing, bouncing, and literally flying; wonder filled every face, young and old. Voices echoed around the massive room as the smell of rubber and chalk wrapped around Ryan.

Scattered around the building were men and women wearing bright yellow T-shirts with 'Adventure Coach' printed on the front and 'Play Yourself Fit' on the back.

Up ahead, John walked on some sort of tightrope, holding his arms above his head for balance. A number of the volunteers from Habitat for Humanity crowded around and spoke excitedly. Smiling, John leaped off the line and landed with both feet on the padded floor. "Our Adventure Coaches will get all you guys hooked up with harnesses, equipment, and some safety rules," he told them. "Just follow them over to the equipment issue area."

Looking up, he saw Ryan. "Hey, buddy, I'm glad you came." He shook Ryan's hand and squeezed his shoulder, then turned. "And you must be Karisa and the rest of the family. Hi, I'm John."

"Mommy, I want to do that." Joy pointed at kids flipping off ten-foot ledges into foam pits.

Karisa tightened her grip on Joy's hand. "I don't know sweetheart, I think that's for the big kids."

"It's an adventure for all ages," said John. "It's perfectly safe and we have some coaches set up to take care of all the kids from the Habitat for Humanity gang. It was the least I could do after all the volunteer work they did." He looked down at Joy. "If your mom says it's okay, that is."

Joy looked at Karisa. "Pleeeease, Mommy."

Karisa looked helplessly at Ryan, who shrugged, then at Jill. "Are you sure it's safe?"

Jill smiled. "Come on, I'll show you. You too Michael, we'll get you set up with the big kids."

Jill grabbed Joy's other hand and maneuvered the group deeper into the chaos.

The quick decision caught Ryan off guard, and he moved to follow, but Karisa looked over her shoulder and mouthed, "I'm okay."

"Let me show you around," John told Ryan.

"Okay, but just quickly, we weren't going to stay long."

"No problem, but don't blame me if I change your mind." John walked Ryan through the maze of people.

"I thought it was a gym," Ryan said.

John nodded. "It started that way, and we still have weights and machines in the back, but they're mostly used for sports-specific training by the members. Most people go to the gym to get more fit, lose weight, or something like that, but those 'New Years' resolutions are seldom completed. We've found that making it fun is the key. All of the activities in the Adventure Gym can accomplish the same thing anyone can do in a regular gym."

John showed him the parkour and trampoline area in the back behind the climbing walls.

"People can take classes—like yoga or aerobics, but even more fun—or work one-on-one with an adventure coach, who helps with specific goals and training; mostly, though, people just come in and play. It's a great way to stay fit, and because they enjoy it so much, they actually stick with it."

"I bet you have your hands full running this place. I'm surprised you have time to volunteer with Habitat."

They were walking through the huge rock climbing area. "You know, when I opened my first gym I was really hands-on. I had to learn the ropes, understand all the pieces of the business. After the first year though, I started promoting my best employees to management and made sure they understood my way of doing things. I gave them guidelines for when to bring me in on the decision process, and I check on all the gyms regularly to make sure everything is running smoothly."

"Gyms? As in more than one?"

"Yeah, I own four in the area."

"Wow, that's amazing!"

"John!"

Ryan turned to see a tall, fit woman run towards them.

"John, we have a problem."

"Diane, meet Ryan."

Out of breath, Diane nodded in Ryan's direction, then when she could speak again, said, "Amy and Bob got in a car accident."

Frowning, John rubbed the back of his neck. "Was anyone hurt?"

"Bob is the one that called. He's bruised up, but Amy broke some ribs, and she's in the hospital right now."

"Thank goodness it wasn't more serious. Jill and I will stop by the hospital."

"Yeah, but we don't have anyone to cover for them on the climbing trip next week."

"Okay, can you find Jill and have her meet me in the office, please?"

Diane nodded and rushed off.

Ryan felt he was intruding, and Karisa had said she wanted to leave early.

"You take care of what you need to John, we need to leave anyway," said Ryan.

John shook his head. "You can come too, Ryan, this shouldn't take long, and then I'll get you set up on some of the activities."

Ryan looked around quickly, trying to find Karisa, but didn't see her anywhere in the mass of people.

"Come on," said John.

Ryan nodded and followed John to the back of the gym, arriving at a door with large windows on both sides. Ryan could see whiteboards with dates and names printed on them and a few computers. Jill and Karisa were already inside with Diane.

Ryan went to Karisa and asked, "Where are the kids?"

She smiled. "Don't worry, they're fine."

Diane was explaining the accident to Jill.

"Are they okay?" asked Jill.

"They're fine," answered Diane. "We're going to have to cancel the climbing trip next week, though."

"Alright, let's not get ahead of ourselves," said John. "Walk me through the problem, Diane, and then tell me how you would solve it if you were me."

"Well, first you'd tell me to breathe. You always tell me to breathe." Diane took a deep breath. "So our two best-qualified guides are not able to lead the climbing trip next week, which leaves you, Jill, and me. Jill is away next week at that conference, you have a speaking engagement here in town, and I have to run the gym. So, we'll have to cancel because we don't have any guides for the trip."

"Maybe," said Jill. "If that's your solution, how do we tell our clients?"

Diane took another deep breath. "Since we can't do the climbs safely, we can explain the problem honestly and hope they'll understand, then offer them a discount if they can delay the trip."

John nodded and looked at Jill.

"I'd give them free passes," said Jill. "It's only five guys, right?"

Diane nodded.

"It's worth it, and it's the right thing to do," Jill said, looking back at John.

"I've got an idea," said John, taking his cell out, selecting a number, and putting it on the table. Then he turned the speaker on so everyone could hear. It rang twice, then a voice answered.

"Cliff's Climbing Place."

"Hey Cliff, this is John Weise."

"John, how are you?"

"Doing good, buddy, but I need a favor. Two of my certified climbing guides just got in a car accident, and I have a climbing trip scheduled out at Yosemite next week. Do you have any experienced guides who can make the trip? I'll pay your guys, and I'll send some of my coaches over to cover for them at your climbing gym if you need help."

"Are your employees okay?" asked Cliff.

"Just banged up I think. I'm going to check on them later."

"Good. Yeah, I got a couple of guys, no problem. Let me look at the calendar and get back to you."

"Awesome! Thanks a lot, Cliff, I owe you one." John hung up.

"You know Cliff?" asked Diane. "I thought he was your competition."

"Jill and I have climbed with him several times. He's good people. Anyway, problem solved. Follow up with Cliff tomorrow and let me know if you need any more help. What hospital are Amy and Bob at? Memorial?"

Diane nodded.

"Alright, Jill and I will give them a call and stop in to see them on the way home." He turned to Ryan and Karisa and smiled. "Let's get you guys geared up."

"That was amazing!" Ryan felt the adrenaline pumping through his body as he landed on the ground, John helping him untie the rope from his climbing harness.

"I'm glad you're having a good time. Like I said earlier, people are way more likely to stay active if they can have fun while they're doing it." Ryan agreed completely, but he also thought that part of what made it so fun was John. The two men had clicked at the Habitat event but didn't have much of a chance to get to know one another. Now, they'd spent the last couple of hours laughing, joking, and talking about their shared taste in movies, all while playing in John's gym. Ryan couldn't remember the last time he'd had so much fun.

On impulse, he blurted out a thought that had been floating around his head all afternoon.

"Would you be my mentor?"

John froze, a slightly stunned expression on his face.

"I hope you're not offended," said Ryan quickly, mentally berating himself for not handling that with a little more finesse.

John shook his head slowly. "No, I'm not offended. Why me?"

"Look, it's okay if you don't—"

"I didn't say that," John interrupted. "Just tell me why. Last weekend you were schmoozing with the senior management at your company so that you could find a mentor. I'd like to know what changed your mind."

Ryan felt the weight of this moment, though he didn't know why. "I—I don't know exactly. It's just…when I look at the leadership at my company, they've been working there for decades. Hell, I've been there over a decade myself. I'm not sure that's what I want to do with my life. I want more money, sure, but I want time with my family too. And, to tell you the truth, when I see you and Jill and hear the way you talk to your employees and help them through problems, how you and your wife work together so seamlessly, it's something—something I think I want, or at least closer to it than what I have now. You know about real estate. You have all this," Ryan gestured at the gym around them, "and yet you still give your wife enough time that she looks at you in a way mine hasn't in a long time. I want to learn from someone who I'd like to be more like, and that's not the leadership team at CaptivSoft. That's someone like you. That's why." Ryan took a breath. "I think."

John nodded slowly. "Okay," he said.

"Okay?" Ryan said, a little stunned at his easy agreement.

"Okay. Let's do this. But I have some conditions."

Conditions? "Sure, okay, what are they?"

"I've mentored several people over the years, and most of the time I've really enjoyed it. It's great to see others transform, grow, and succeed. What has driven me crazy in the past, though, is when I offer to mentor someone, and they end up always complaining about life, what they are not good at, what's wrong with the world, and they have nothing but excuses for why they didn't do what they said they would do. But I don't think that's you, Ryan. You seem optimistic, willing to hear feedback, and I feel that you are committed to doing what you say you will do. Am I right?"

Ryan nodded his head. "I'm definitely committed. I just want to learn and be the best provider for my family that I can be."

"Great, so I'm happy to mentor you, but here are my conditions. One, you are willing to be real with me, be fully transparent, and you will do what you say you will do. Two, you take full responsibility for your results and your life and don't complain, whine, or act like a victim. And three, you are willing to have fun."

"What do you mean, willing to have fun?"

"We can look at challenges as problems and complain about them, or we can look at challenges as adventures and face them with creativity and positivity. It's all about mindset. Are you willing to focus on the latter?"

"That sounds fair."

"Also, I don't want our mentoring sessions to be boring, sitting at a desk or just talking on the phone. I want to get outside and play. You can learn more about a person in an hour of play than in a lifetime of conversation. Plato supposedly said that, but whether it was him or someone else, it doesn't matter; I agree with that statement completely. Every week I usually get outside on my own to enjoy some type of playful adventure—hiking, mountain biking, paddling, whatever. I think it would be fun for you to come along, and we can do our mentoring sessions while we play. Sound good?"

"Sounds great!"

"Okay, let's start tomorrow morning, early. I'll text you the details and directions. Just remember to dress for adventure!"

They walked to one of the foam pits where kids were climbing and jumping. Karisa and Jill sat on a bench to the side chatting animatedly. Guilt spiked in Ryan's chest as his mind once again drifted back to his secret. He took a deep breath. John was his mentor now, and he invested in real estate. Maybe he could put Ryan's mind at ease. If

Ryan could just be sure that he had done the right thing, telling Karisa would be so much easier.

"You mentioned that you don't like flipping, can I ask why?"

"I don't have anything against flipping, it's a great way to make money if you like that sort of thing. I just meant that I wouldn't consider it my type of investing—it's more of a full-time job. I prefer passive real estate investments that make me money without taking up so much of my time."

"I guess that makes sense. I don't really have time to add anything else to my plate either, but I really want to learn to make money through real estate. I actually just signed up for Roy Clark's three-day course. It's about flipping, but hopefully, I learn something worthwhile. Especially considering how much I paid for it." Ryan rubbed the back of his neck anxiously, his mind once again on what Karisa would think.

"Hmm… Well, I'm certainly not here to tell you how to live your life, but I'm not sure spending your money on a course was the way to go. There's no 'secret' to real estate investing, all of that information is free online and in books. Make sure you research the seminar, there are a lot of scammers out there."

Ryan's gut clenched, nausea building with each word out of John's mouth. It was something that had been weighing on his mind since he gave the Roy Clark people his money. Now, not only had he lied to Karisa, but instead of investing that money in their future, he might have actually thrown it away.

Ryan glanced over to where his wife sat, smiling and chatting happily while watching the kids climb and play. Would she ever forgive him?

———————————

Once they got home that night, Ryan was exhausted. His muscles ached in ways he hadn't felt in a long time. He carried Joy, already fast asleep, in from the car. When Ryan checked on Michael, he had already collapsed on top of his covers, snoring, and he hadn't even taken off his shoes. With an amused grin, Ryan headed to his office.

His brief last week had gone brilliantly. Howard had complimented him almost every day. And they had another one coming up. It would definitely mean a lot of late hours for the rest of the week. A lot of missed soccer games. More time away from the family. All for the promotion, because that was the goal. Right?

Karisa hugged him from behind, kissing him on the cheek. "I had a good time today."

"I'm glad. Me too." He turned his head to kiss her properly. Guilt washed over him. John's talk today had made him realize his mistake.

"Coming to bed?" she asked.

"In a minute."

She paused. "Something wrong? You look like you want to say something."

"Uh, no. Just tired." He needed to call tonight to get the money back.

She kissed him again. "Don't be long." Then, she turned and left.

He called the Roy Clark hotline number and was put on hold.

While he listened to the elevator music, he thought about John. Ryan hoped that working with John would really set them on the right track, but if he didn't get their money back then there might not be anything that could be done. Karisa wouldn't want to risk the rest of their savings.

An agent came on. Ryan explained his situation and she explained that refunds were only offered for the first twenty-four hours. He had missed the window. There would be no refund of his $5,000.

As the phone disconnected, he felt lost. If he didn't get the promotion, then he would never make their savings back. He had to think of the baby.

A text dinged on his phone.

John: *State Park, 6 am.*

Some directions followed.

Should he just cancel? What was the point?

Ryan sighed. No, he should tell John in person at least.

CHAPTER
SIX

Ryan sleepily pulled into the crowded state park parking lot at 6 am and glanced around, trying to spot John.

Who are these crazy people getting up this early? he chuckled. *Besides me, that is.*

He parked beside a new, futuristic-looking pickup truck and got out to gawk while finishing his second chocolate donut.

What the hell is that?

It was all angles, with huge tires and a bed with a metal cover that slid down diagonally from the cab. *I bet that cost a pretty penny*, he thought. *Someone must be compensating.*

Ryan leaned against his car, still admiring the odd sleekness of the truck, and thought about what to tell John. He would just tell it to him straight, that it just wasn't a good time for him to start investing.

His phone vibrated.

John: *Follow the trail marked Tattoo Point. I'll meet you there.*

Ryan looked around until he found the trail and got started. Though the sun had yet to break over the horizon, the ambient light lit the forest enough for him to see. Before long, Ryan began to breathe harder as the path kept climbing.

He really needed to get back in shape.

He began to parallel a river, and soon Ryan could hear a waterfall in the near distance. Suddenly, he came to a flat, concrete platform about eighty feet long, ending in a cliff with an incredible view of a lush valley. He stood there for a moment. John stood by the cliff, facing away from him. Graffiti completely covered the concrete between them: vibrant oranges, reds, and greens overlapped each other with everything from what looked like professional spray paint art to amateur scribbles and quotes about lost love and frustration.

Ryan slowly walked toward John, reading the different quotes that people had felt the need to share.

'I guess we'll never know if we never try.'

'May your choices reflect your hopes, not your fears.'

Two ropes, each attached to three separate metal anchors in the concrete, disappeared over the edge. Ryan looked down and saw the ends blending into a waterfall caused by the river, which threw water into the air before crashing into a bluish-green pond eighty feet below.

As if on cue, the sun rose above the horizon, a bright yellow ball surrounded by oranges and soft aqua blues.

"Nice place you got here, John," said Ryan.

John turned, smiled, then shook Ryan's hand before pulling him in for a hug.

"I love to come up to this old dam in the morning to catch the sunrise," said John, turning back to face the sun.

A mild breeze blew, cooling the sweat on Ryan's face, sweat he hadn't realized was there until now. "What are we doing here, John?" Ryan asked, his voice cracking a little. His palms felt wet.

"Did you bring an extra set of clothes like I asked?"

Ryan backed away from the edge. "Look, John, I've never done this before. I'm not so sure about this."

"Hi, Ryan," said a familiar voice.

Bridgette walked up as Ryan turned, her ponytail bobbing behind her. She carried a helmet in one hand and wore a harness over her shorts and floral one-piece swimsuit.

"Are you rappelling with us too? It's fantastic!" As she stepped up beside them, Ryan noticed water dripping from her hair onto the concrete.

"Um…"

John clapped Ryan on the back. "I invited the Jonas family this morning too, just something else to celebrate their new house. I think seeing the sunrise in all this splendor is a good way to make new beginnings."

"Can I go again?" asked Bridgette.

"Sure thing, let me get you hooked up."

They walked over to one of the ropes, and Ryan followed in a daze.

John checked the rope and the anchor points, then routed the rope through the braking device attached to her harness. She buckled on her helmet and backed up to the edge.

"Remember to release your break hand gradually," said John.

"I will, thanks." Slowly, she disappeared over the cliff until Ryan couldn't see her anymore.

John turned. "Ready?"

Ryan stuck his head over and watched as Bridgette deftly maneuvered her way down, finally fading out of view into the waterfall. He wiped his hands on his pants, taking a deep breath.

"Calm down, buddy," said John. "You're inside your head."

Ryan turned toward the sound of John's reassuring voice. "I think that's understandable since you want me to dive off a cliff."

"It's completely safe, I promise you," John picked up a harness. "Take a deep breath. There's a Gremlin in each one of us."

"Gremlin? What's that?"

"It's what I call the embodiment of all our fears and doubts, the whispers in our mind that say: 'You can't do that', 'You're not good enough', or 'You don't deserve that'. We all have them. It's that inner voice that holds us back, and it holds power over us until we bring it into the light. You have to tame your Gremlin and get into the right mindset to move toward what you want." He threw the harness and Ryan reflexively caught it. "Once you step outside your comfort zone, then you can get to the solutions you need."

Looking over the edge, Ryan saw the rope mingling with the spray of the waterfall and felt a momentary loss of equilibrium, then stepped back to safety.

"It's okay, relax," said John. "Breathe."

Ryan did. "Let's do this before I change my mind."

John smiled. "Great, I'll get you hooked up." John talked through the process of putting on the harness while he attached the rope and demonstrated the breaking procedures. It all went by in a flash, and then Ryan was leaning back into nothingness. "Keep your L shape, you're doing great."

Ryan hadn't taken his first step yet. His feet remained glued to the side of the concrete platform that stretched about six feet below him, his legs straight and shaking slightly. He bent ninety degrees at the waist with his head just above the platform and level with John's boots. "I don't know if I can do this, John." His legs quaked more.

"Ryan, you got this. Don't let your Gremlin talk you out of this. Bend your knees a bit. Remember, your right hand is your break hand, so don't take it off the rope. Release gradually. Look at where your feet are and where they're going."

Ryan looked at his feet. A spray-painted depiction of a purple monster stared back at him from beneath his shoes. *So that's what a Gremlin looks like*, he thought. He released his brake hand slowly and moved one foot down, followed by the next.

"There you go buddy, nothing to it."

Ryan began to read the quotes written on the cement as he slowly walked past them.

'Johnny loves Jenny.'

But do you still Johnny? Ryan thought, smiling as the butterflies diminished in his stomach with each step.

'What you pay attention to becomes your life.'

You can bet I'm paying attention right now.

The concrete ended, and he felt the rougher texture of uneven rock beneath his shoes. He made his way slowly downward, gaining confidence with each step until he stopped right above where the waterfall met the rope. Cold droplets sprayed onto his shoes and the bottom of his pants.

Ryan froze, staring down at the water falling into the pond below.

"Ryan, look at me." Suddenly, John appeared beside him on a separate rope.

Ryan turned his head.

"You're safe, nothing is going to happen. I checked your equipment. There's no going back. Breathe in courage and keep moving."

Ryan looked back at his feet and released the brake, stepping into the froth. He gasped, feeling the cold needles hit his face and arms as he descended, then he burst through the flow and crossed the rest of the distance to a shallow pool at the bottom. He walked the last steps into the waist-deep water and ducked his head underneath before coming up with a gasp.

"Look out below!"

Ryan looked up, and John descended from above attached to the rope on his right side, splashing into the pond.

John helped Ryan unhook from the rope. "How do you feel?"

"Awesome!" That's all Ryan could think of to describe the experience. "So awesome!"

"Want to go again?"

_____

Ryan and the Jonas family went down twice more, then Bridgette and her family said their goodbyes with wet hugs, and Ryan helped coil the rope.

"Thanks for inviting me, John, that was one of the most amazing things I've ever done."

"No problem, Ryan," said John. "You know why I brought you out here?"

"To scare the bejesus out of me?"

John laughed. "That's part of it."

"What do you mean?"

"I wanted to shock you out of your own head."

John sounded sincere, something Ryan wasn't accustomed to hearing. It reassured him in a way that he couldn't put his finger on. Unsure how to respond, he chuckled uncertainly.

They finished putting the equipment into a backpack, then John inspected the rope and laid it on the cement. "Sit down for a minute, let's talk."

Ryan sat on the cement, legs hanging over the cliff he'd just rappelled down.

They both watched the sun rise over the canyon. His wet clothes left Ryan a little chilly, but the bright, clear skies hinted at higher temperatures to come.

"You asked me to mentor you, so here's your first session."

"I'm not sure you're going to be able to help me much, John," Ryan interrupted. "I basically don't have any money to invest since I spent it on that seminar."

"You asked me to mentor you because you thought I could help, that hasn't changed. My advice is free, except for a couple of rappels down the cliff. So, let's just look at your situation and take it one day at a time."

"Well, I spent $5,000 on that real estate seminar last week, and they wouldn't give me a refund. I didn't go because I'm still hoping the bank will be able to reverse the charge, but I'm becoming more convinced that I'm not getting that money back. So, I didn't have a lot of money to invest in the first place, but now I'm even worse off."

John nodded. "Ryan, I know this looks bad, and I'm so sorry you're going through this. I've made some mistakes in the past and went through some tough times, so I truly understand how you're feeling right now. I know you'll get through this. The truth is, you'll learn and grow. You'll begin to see things differently. Over time these small, incremental changes will create a big mindset shift. All of a sudden you'll look at money in a whole new way. That mindset shift will have an exponential effect on your life. It will change how you see things, and then everything will start to change."

"I agree, John, I'm obviously doing something wrong. Something has to change."

John paused, then asked, "What did Karisa say?"

Ryan's breath caught. His chest tightened as the vise of fear and shame slowly crushed his heart. *What do I say to her?* he thought. "I haven't told her yet."

John nodded slowly. "You have to tell her, Ryan," he said. "You guys are partners. I know it hurts, believe me, I do, but you have to do it. These things only get worse with time, never better."

They were both quiet for a time. Ryan enjoyed the sun on his face. "Do you really think you can help me?"

"Everyone's situation is unique," said John. "Let's start at the basics. I need you to list out all your income, liabilities, and assets. Write them down, including all of your expenses, day to day, for the last thirty days."

Ryan whistled. "That's going to take a while."

"Let's start there, Ryan. Trust me, this will all make sense. We'll talk about your cash flow next time. How does a week sound?"

"I think I can get it done by then."

"Okay, now on to the mentoring."

"Isn't the cash flow data the mentoring?" Ryan asked.

"That's a piece of it. Over the next couple of months, I want to share several key lessons with you. Your personal financial situation and the management of your liabilities play a part, and we'll talk about that next time once you've done the work, but the first thing I want to discuss with you is your mindset."

"Shocking me, I get it. Mission accomplished."

"That was the first step. Now, we have to dig a little deeper." John turned his head to look at Ryan. "What do you want, Ryan?"

Ryan paused. "What do you mean?"

"Yesterday, you were very frank with me. You told me you weren't satisfied with the direction of your life. So, what would make you happy? What would have to change for you to be happy?"

"I think getting that promotion for one thing," Ryan said quickly.

"You mentioned that before, but be careful not to put all your focus on making more money. If you don't change your habits, it's doubtful your financial situation will actually change. And you need to understand your habits now in order to do that."

Ryan laughed. "Surely making more money is a step in the right direction though."

"But what will that money bring you?" said John. "Will it bring you real wealth?"

"Real wealth? What's that? Like stocks and real estate, things like that?"

"That's all part of it of course, but true wealth is more than the physical forms you're talking about. It does include earning enough income to cover your expenses, building financial reserves, investing, and making that money grow. But real wealth is actually investing your money in experiences that will bring you and your family true happiness. It's the ability to live life on your own terms. It's about having the money and freedom to do what you want, when you want, with the people you want to be with, and most importantly, to enjoy each moment."

Ryan paused to dwell on that. "That's very Gandhi-ish," he finally said.

John smiled. "It is health that is real wealth and not pieces of gold or silver. That's Gandhi."

"Sounds like you called me fat."

John glanced at Ryan's midsection with a lopsided grin.

"Hey!"

"You said it, I didn't." John stood up, shouldering the equipment bag, and handing the rope to Ryan. "Come on, let's get this gear back to the truck."

They set off down the trail at a brisk walk.

I'm not that out of shape, am I? thought Ryan. He watched John, who kept a brisk pace and continued breathing easily as Ryan struggled to keep up. *Okay, so I could do with a little more exercise.*

At the parking lot, Ryan saw the cover to the back of the futuristic truck begin to retract as they approached.

"This is yours?" asked Ryan.

"Yeah, great truck. Eco-friendly and still has tons of power. Definitely one of my best investments."

They threw the equipment into the back and John turned to Ryan.

"So, have you thought more about what you want?"

"I think I just have to earn more money. Then everything will come together."

"Why do you want more money?"

"Well, that's where all my problems stem from. We have debt, we want to retire someday, we want to save for the kids' college. All of that takes money."

"I see. Have you ever heard of Tal-Ben Shahar?"

Ryan shook his head.

"He's a philosopher and former professor at Harvard. One of his most famous quotes is: 'Happiness is not about making it to the peak of the mountain nor is it about climbing aimlessly around the mountain; *happiness is the experience of climbing toward the peak.'* One of Harvard's most popular classes was the one he gave on happiness. The bottom line is that humans are happier when we are moving toward our most important goals."

The back of the truck bed began to close.

"So, Ryan, what needs to change for you to be happy? Is it just more money?"

Ryan thought about that and couldn't come up with an answer.

"We'll get to making money, I promise," said John. "But if you keep doing what you've always done, the results will be the same. So there has to be some change. Einstein said that 'The definition of insanity is doing the same thing over and over again but expecting different results.' Those cash flow records will show us some of your habits, and then we can decide the best way to change them. I want you to remember that more money doesn't necessarily lead to happiness, but true happiness leads to more *real* wealth. Got it?"

Ryan nodded automatically. "I think so."

"So, here's your homework," said John, reaching into the cab of the truck.

"More homework?"

"You have to work to make changes." He handed Ryan a tan moleskin notebook with the word *Grow* printed in white on the front.

Ryan leafed through the empty notebook.

"I want you to imagine yourself three years from today. Write down what you look like, what you're doing, and how you are living. See yourself the way you want to be. How have you changed? Are you happier? Why or why not?"

"I'm more concerned about the present right now."

John shrugged. "What do you have to lose?"

"Fair enough." Ryan reached out and John shook his hand. "John, thanks for today. I don't know if all this will help me get where I want to be, but I'll give it a try." Ryan returned to his car. His clothes were nearly dry, so he decided not to change. He started the car and backed up to leave. The day's events filled his mind, from the rappelling and the advice to the notebook. Would all of this help him?

John pulled up next to him and motioned for him to roll down his window. "One more thing," said John.

"What's that?" Ryan asked.

John smiled. "Just breathe."

———————

That night, after a long day of work, Ryan pulled into his driveway, turned the car off, and put his head against the steering wheel. Telling John about his situation had lifted a great weight from his shoulders, but he dreaded the next moment. He remembered John's question. *"What did Karisa say?"*

What do I say to her? he thought again.

A light appeared in the kitchen window, bringing Ryan back to the present. He took a long ragged breath, locked up the car, and walked into the house.

"Hey, hun," Karisa greeted him warmly. The air had lingering odors of chicken and rice. "I saved you some dinner, let me warm it up."

She stood there, looking beautiful in purple yoga pants and a loose black T-shirt, hair in a ponytail, a plate of food in one hand, and a dishtowel in the other.

Her smile changed. "What's wrong?" she asked.

He put his backpack on the table and stood in front of her.

"I made a mistake," he told her quietly.

She stood there, frozen in place, as he explained the seminar and money he had spent. Her face changed from shock to anger and then something he didn't recognize, something he had never seen before. Betrayal?

"Say something," he said when he had finished.

She shook her head once, then tried to put the plate on the counter but missed, and it crashed into the tile floor. She stared at him, then turned and walked away, slamming the garage door.

At first, he didn't move. He didn't know what to do. He wanted to explain more, how he had done it all for their family, for their future. He walked quickly to the door and stopped.

Through the heavy wood door, he could hear her sobs.

CHAPTER
SEVEN

His desk phone rang, startling Ryan from his thoughts.

"Got a moment to join me in my office?" asked Howard.

"Of course, let me secure my workstation real quick."

Five minutes later, he knocked on Howard's office door.

"Come in, Ryan, have a seat."

"What's going on?"

Howard held out a can of Coke, but Ryan shook his head. "Well, I just wanted to touch base with you. Everyone was really impressed with your presentation last week, as you know. A couple of the senior management guys mentioned speaking to you at the Habitat for Humanity gig a couple of weeks ago. Have you talked to one of them about mentorship?"

Ryan heard Howard speaking, but struggled to process the words. What was the point of any of this? John was right—money was a means to an end, not the objective itself. The objective was to provide for his family. What good was working toward a promotion when Karisa wouldn't even speak to him?

"Ryan?"

"Sorry, I just had to think about it for a second, but the answer is no, I haven't sought out mentorship from one of them."

"Okay, well, figure it out fast. The decision for the promotion is coming up in the next few months, and one of those guys taking you under their wing could be the thing that tips the scales."

Should he tell Howard about John? It would at least be controversial.

"Well, I have decided on a mentor from outside the company. A man by the name of John Weise."

Howard paused, obviously surprised, then asked, "The guy at the charity house-building thing? Why would you choose him?"

"Well, I don't know," stuttered Ryan. "He and I just clicked. I liked his attitude and outlook. He seems like a good guy."

Howard ran a hand through his hair with a sigh. "Ryan, the whole reason I asked you to seek mentorship was so your mentor could speak up on your behalf during the vote. John Weise doesn't have a vote here. "

"I hadn't considered that…"

"Well, consider it now. You need to choose a mentor who is going to help you get what you want out of life."

Ryan nodded absently. What did he want out of life? Did he need a mentor who could help improve his work at the company and assist him in getting the promotion? *Choose a mentor who is going to help you get what you want out of life.* What did he really want?

––––––––––––

Ryan sat in his home office with all the cashflow documents he'd assembled at John's request. Karisa was in their room. There hadn't been much conversation ever since…

He'd purposefully been coming home from work late all week in order to avoid the awkward silence, so he'd barely seen Michael and Joy. Sometimes there were leftovers in the fridge, sometimes not. The door to their bedroom stayed closed in the evenings, so he began sleeping on the floor in his office so as not to upset the kids in the morning. When he did catch sight of Karisa, on that rare occasion, she said nothing, just stared at him briefly and moved on to whatever she was doing.

He sighed. He had to fix this.

Ryan looked at the notebook John had given him.

Grow.

What did that even mean?

At the top of the first page, John had written a quote: *If you take care of the minutes, the years will take care of themselves —Rick Hanson.*

Well, at least it wasn't Ghandi calling him fat again.

Ryan jotted down notes about mindset and his Gremlin.

He thought about yesterday. On the inside cover, he wrote REAL WEALTH. John had said that real wealth was about more than just money, but Ryan was pretty sure that more money would still solve most of his problems. However, he googled Tal-Ben Shahar and spent some time reading about happiness, taking more notes.

He turned to a clean page and wrote expenses.

He spread all the documents out. He'd told John that he'd give it a try. Eventually, he'd put all this into an excel sheet, but for now, Ryan just wanted to get an idea of where all the money was going. He started transcribing all the data.

As he wrote out everything the family had spent over the last month, he started to note trends, highlighting them in the same color so he could add them up at the end.

$125 at Starbucks. How was that possible? It wasn't like they went there every day, but he had to admit that he and Karisa did have a soft spot for their mocha Frappuccinos. Still, it seemed like a lot.

He moved on.

Boat payment: $500. Two car payments: $1,100.

Almost $600 for restaurant delivery. They really should cook more.

Another $500 eating out, if you could call it that. It wasn't even good restaurants—McDonald's, Wendy's, and KFC mostly.

About $700 from Hobby Lobby. What was that about? He'd have to ask Karisa—when she started speaking to him again.

Netflix, Hulu, Apple TV, HBO Max, and Disney+ ate up another $75. He couldn't remember the last time he'd had time to watch television.

In the end, he was kind of disgusted with their spending habits.

He added up their credit card bills, the mortgage, some estimations of their monthly food and utility bills, and felt a little faint. The total alarmed him, especially considering a good part of their savings was gone now. *Thanks to me*, he thought.

He wrote down the Einstein quote in the notebook. *Insanity is doing the same thing over and over.* Obviously, the change would be the promotion. They could make some spending changes, but he didn't think that would make a huge difference.

He wrote down, *Who is my future self?* Who was he in the future? The same, promoted, making more money. Was that change? He wasn't sure. He tapped the notebook, then put his pen down and picked up his phone.

He sent a text to John.

Ryan: *Accounts done, do you want me to send them to you?*

Within seconds, he received a text from John.

John: *No need, let's talk. 6:00 am tomorrow.*

Directions followed.

John: *Dress for adventure.*

Ryan googled the directions. *Where the heck is John taking me now?* He closed his eyes and ran his hands through his hair. He felt Karisa's presence and turned. She stood in the doorway, hands on her flat stomach, staring at him with blank eyes.

"Hey, babe," he started.

She seemed to focus on him, actually see him, for a second, then turned and walked away.

He wiped tears from his eyes, and one landed on the notebook, smearing the words 'future self.'

On the inside cover of the notebook, beside REAL WEALTH, Ryan added a single word.

Freedom.

Who was his future self?

Prepared for his family's future. Honest with his wife. More time for his kids.

He wiped his eyes again and sniffed.

Changed.

Happy.

CHAPTER EIGHT

"Can I help you?" asked the Starbucks barista.

"Yeah, could I have a Venti Mocha Frap…" Ryan paused. "You know, could I just have a bottle of water, please?" *Two bucks for water? Less than the Frappuccino at least.*

The work he had done last night on his expenses had really opened his eyes to his finances. He'd never looked at it in such detail.

His cell buzzed.

John: *Outside.*

Ryan walked up to John's truck, the same fancy, futuristic one he'd seen at the state park. Two bikes were strapped in the back and the windows were down.

"Hop in." John wore sunglasses pushed back on his head.

"Just a minute," Ryan said, then grabbed a backpack from his car and jumped into the passenger side. "Where'd you get the bike, do you have a supply at the gym or something?"

"Nah, it's my son's. It should work okay for you though. You look about his size."

"How old is your son?"

"He's forty-five, but he left this bike at my house so we can ride when he's here. He has another one up in Colorado that he uses with his family."

What the hell? "Did you just say your son is forty-five? John, how old are you?"

John laughed. "Sixty-eight."

"Shut up! No way you are sixty-eight."

"Yep." John put it in drive and took off down the road.

No way, Ryan thought. He stole glances at John. *Just, no way.*

"So, how did you do with the expenses?" asked John.

"I won't lie, it surprised me. I couldn't believe how much we spent on eating out and delivery, among other things. Do you want to see everything? I brought copies." Ryan patted his backpack.

John shook his head. "Most people have no idea what they're spending money on until they do a deep dive into their accounts like you did. The information is for you and Karisa to use."

"What do we do with it?" Ryan took a swallow of water.

"I want you to look at every dollar you spend and analyze it. Do you need to spend that money? Does it make you happy? Is there a cheaper way to do it?"

"Seems like we're nickel and diming," said Ryan.

"I've seen people cut over thirty percent of their expenses when they did the work and spent the time looking deep."

"Thirty percent! You're kidding."

John glanced over at Ryan. "Everyone's situation is different. All I'm asking is for you to take an honest look at each item you purchase and evaluate if you need to do that next month. I bet you can cut at least twenty percent."

Ryan laughed out loud. "I really don't know if that's possible."

"That sounds a little negative. Could that be your Gremlin talking right now?" asked John.

My Gremlin? Why am I resisting this so hard? Ryan looked at the water bottle in his hand. *Could I cut that much if I tried?*

"Only you know what's important to you and your family, Ryan," said John, turning off the main road in the direction of a sign that said 'Backbone Trail.'

"I'll take a look and see, but I'm not sure it's going to help me in the long run. How much does it take to get involved in real estate investing?" asked Ryan.

"That depends. Basically, you'll need around thirty thousand to get started."

Ryan sighed. "I don't see how I could get started any time soon. It took over ten years for us to save our emergency fund of $20,000, and now we have less than that. What about 'other people's money'? I've heard people use that term a lot."

"Only if it brings a higher return than it costs. We'll talk about how to do that using leverage, but first, let's focus on your liabilities and assets. You need to be aware and honest with yourself about how you're spending money. Liabilities are everything from financial debt on depreciating assets to bad habits. The only good debt is debt that brings a higher return than it costs. If something provides income, better health, happiness or time, it's an asset. If something costs you money, health, happiness, or time, it's a liability. It's pretty simple."

"I don't think it's that black and white,' said Ryan.

"You'd be surprised. If you cut $2,000 a month in expenses, in ten months you could start investing in real estate. How much did you pay for that water?"

"Two bucks."

"Most people make several impulse buys every day like magazines, smoothies, coffees. Maybe they buy lunch instead of bringing it from home. How much do you think you spend on that?"

Ryan thought for a second. "I don't know, about $10 or $15."

"Do you need them? Is it something you could pass on or bring from home?"

Ryan thought. "Probably."

"So, let's call that $10 a day, $300 a month. Double that for Karisa is $600 a month. $6,000 in ten months. That's something simple. If you cut other things, every little bit helps."

"It just seems petty."

"Ryan, there's nothing petty about saving for your future, it's about the choices you make every day. Here's another one. Are you making payments on your car?"

"Yeah, I have three more years on the loan."

"What are your payments?"

"Around $500 a month."

"If you traded that in for a used car, no payments, you'd save another $5,000 over ten months. You're halfway there. It's just transportation, right? But the money you'd save can be put to work to secure your future."

Ryan thought about what John was saying. They needed Karisa's SUV for the kids, but his BMW, he really just used it for work—and to look cool.

John pulled into a parking lot. "We're here."

They both got out and began unloading the bikes.

John handed Ryan a helmet.

"You know, everyone's journey is different, but a change in life does require a change in the way you think," said John.

Ryan buckled his helmet. "Sounds like Yoda stuff again."

"Well, I do believe that what we focus on determines our reality. It's about mindset. Everyone makes mistakes. We can learn from those mistakes or we can dwell on them.

It depends on what kind of future reality you want to create." He swung his leg over the bike.

I'm not sure I have much of a future if Karisa never forgives me, Ryan thought. He mounted his bike. "I've never ridden off-road, how do I not crack my skull? Any advice before we get started?"

"Yeah, remember that the left lever is the front brake, so don't squeeze it too hard or you'll go OTB."

"OTB? Is that a technical term? What does that mean?"

"Yeah, a technical term for why we wear helmets." John laughed. "It means 'Over the Bars'." He took off down the trail and Ryan followed.

They traveled at a moderate pace along trails ranging from wide sandy fire breaks to narrow dirt paths that mostly rose and fell gradually. Ryan kept up easily, enjoying the scenery of reddish-tan sandstone formations and greenery. Occasionally, the trail ran along the side of a hill, and he could see caves and crevices on the other side of the valley. After about an hour, they climbed for a long stretch and Ryan put the bike in the lowest gear. John started to get ahead, despite Ryan's attempts to close the distance, and soon disappeared around a corner. When he finally reached the top, Ryan saw a huge boulder that seemed to have been split by some giant's axe, the two sides separated, and John stood between them looking over a cliff.

Each breath required herculean effort as Ryan pedaled the last few yards and parked beside John's bike. His shirt stuck to his chest and his hair was plastered to the side of his face when he walked over to stand at the edge of the cliff.

A mix of forest and beautiful tan rock stretched out across the valley below. From their elevated vantage point, Ryan could see other hikers moving up and down the terrain. Across from where they stood, a giant boulder balanced almost magically on a pointed stone in a way that appeared as if a gentle breeze could topple it.

"That's a nice view," said Ryan. He stared intently at the cliff face in front of him below the teetering rock. "Are people climbing over there?"

"Yes, it's a popular climbing spot. That guy is climbing a route called Sunset Bouldervard. It's a pretty difficult route, but some of the other climbs on that cliff are good for beginners."

Ryan enjoyed the light breeze and watched the climbers. *Those cliffs are straight up and those people are nuts.* "Do you teach that kind of climbing?" he asked.

John nodded, swallowing some water. "Sure. You can learn most of the basic skills at the gym. You could come to our fitness class in the morning if you want. They always work on some climbing skills during the session and you can get into some formal training later if you are interested."

"How much is it? Not sure it's in my budget."

"That's the right attitude. Don't worry about it though, I'll give you a one-month free pass, see if you like it. It's not for everyone."

"Thanks, John. You don't have to, I know you're running a business."

"It's no problem. We have an ongoing promotion and the business runs itself at this point, so it's no additional work for me."

"Runs itself? Don't be so modest, that place probably takes a lot of your time. Especially four gyms, I can't even imagine."

John shook his head. "Not really, I have a great team running the gyms. The key is to create systems, train the right people, and make a clear process that everyone follows. That frees up my time to focus on what I'm best at and love doing, which benefits everyone. Sure, I check in on all the gyms to make sure everything is going smoothly, but for the last few years it's been pretty hands-off."

"I can't believe you have all this free time. I barely have time to breathe. John, you have to help me organize my life better. Even coming out here, if it wasn't early in the morning, I'd be stuck between family and work."

"It's all about balance, Ryan, like riding a bike. Did you bring your notebook?"

Ryan pulled it out of his backpack and handed it over, then followed John over to a stone picnic table. John opened to the next blank page. He drew a circle with five lines intersecting in the middle so that it looked like a pizza cut into ten equal slices. He then labeled each slice: Career, Finance, Possessions, Health and Fitness, Fun and Recreation, Personal Growth and Education, Friends, Family, Romance, and Spiritual.

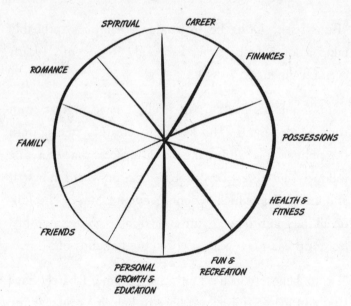

"Here's a way to check out how you feel about your life. It's all about how satisfied *you* are with these different areas, not anyone else. Assess these on a scale of zero to ten, ten being awesome and zero meaning super unhappy." John handed the notebook back.

Ryan paused at career. "Well, I seem to be in a good place to get that promotion, but I spend so much time working it really doesn't make me that happy. I'm always stressed that I'm not spending time on other things."

"Okay, focus on just that area for now. Are you happy with the work you do and with your work environment?"

Ryan's pen hovered over the slice. "I mean, I love coding, but I don't always agree with everything they have us do there, or how they make us do it. I'm also not really sure I want to do this the rest of my life. I think I'd like to go into business for myself. I'm hoping that my promotion…"

"You're really overthinking this. How satisfied are you right now, at this moment?"

Ryan felt frustrated. "I'd say it's about a 5 or a 6. Can I put 5.5?" John nodded and Ryan wrote down 5.5 in the slice. He went through the rest of the diagram, filling some quickly and pausing to debate others internally.

When he was finished, he gave the notebook back to John.

John drew lines on the diagram. "Your numbers are represented here as a percentile from the center to the outer rim. Most of your values are around five or six, but you have two that are really low. If that was a wheel, how bumpy would that be? Would you have made it up that hill?"

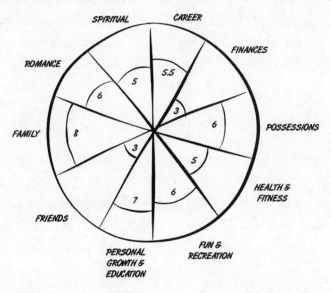

"Probably not, but I'm not sure what you're getting at. I thought you were mentoring me with my financial problems. What do fun, fitness, romance, and friends have to do with that?" asked Ryan. John's cryptic messages frustrated him. Not to mention, the muscle fatigue he felt forced him to recognize that his fitness was a little lower than he had originally rated it.

"It's all connected, Ryan. Let me show you. Close your eyes and lift your right foot."

Ryan did so and extended his arms like a hawk catching an updraft.

"Notice what your body is doing. Feel it," said John.

"I feel like I'm about to fall over," muttered Ryan, tottering.

"But you're not tipping over," Ryan heard John say beside him. "Notice the small corrections your body is making. When you start to lose your balance, it makes larger adjustments. Even when you feel like you are perfectly balanced, your body still makes small corrections. Feel all those little muscles that are working to keep you vertical. You're balancing."

Ryan breathed and teetered less.

"Okay, you can open your eyes."

Ryan did.

John continued. "Balancing life is about noticing when you are leaning too far into one part of your life, and then consciously moving toward another in order to keep from falling. Sometimes those adjustments are small and other times they're big. You need to stay aware of which way you are tipping and keep moving into other areas. If you keep leaning toward only one area, you'll fall on your face."

Ryan looked at his life wheel. "So, you're saying that if I don't improve my fitness, then I'm going to topple over?"

"If you don't take care of your health, you could lose everything. But once you begin to improve your satisfaction in the areas of your life that don't seem to be working for you, you'll see that all the other areas begin to work better too.

Ryan bit his lip. He wanted to be honest, but he didn't want to upset John. "John, it sounds like a bunch of mumbo jumbo. I'm sorry, I'm just having trouble seeing past my financial issues right now."

"If you only focus on your finances, you're not going to achieve real wealth. If you're not clear on where you are in life, you can't change your course to get where you want to be. No clarity, no change. Don't believe anything I say on blind faith. Try improving what you're eating and staying active and see if it works for you. I think you'll find that focusing on small, incremental changes in every area is the way to go. With reference to your finances, breaking down your expenses will move you from thinking 'That's just the way it is.' to 'What other options do I have?'. Spend the next month cutting some of your expenses back, and next time we'll talk about what you can do with that money."

"Okay, I'll give it a shot."

"Be patient, change usually doesn't happen overnight. Ready for your homework?"

"I thought cutting my expenses was the homework."

"Just one more thing. I want you to list your strengths and also those underdeveloped skills that you want to work on, at least three of each. Karisa can help—maybe it will bring your romance score up."

"I don't think Karisa is ready to forgive me yet. We're not talking much right now."

John paused. "You'll probably have to give her time, but it won't hurt to ask. Use the wheel to help you. Then, we'll work on strengthening the skills that are lacking." John stood up. "Small adjustments. That's the way big changes happen. Ready to head back?"

Ryan stood too and stretched. "Ready as I'll ever be."

"Good," said John. "Race you!"

CHAPTER
NINE

When Ryan returned from mountain biking, he saw an unfamiliar white car in front of the house.

It was late. Ryan could hear voices in the garage as he foraged for leftovers in the fridge, but he only recognized Karisa's voice. Laughter, something he hadn't heard in the house lately, drifted through the closed door. He made a sandwich and went to his office.

Opening his grow notebook, Ryan wrote the word 'balance' over the life wheel John had drawn. He laid out paper copies of their debit and credit card statements, spreading all the documents out across his desk. Ryan reviewed his lists, looking for places he could cut.

Ryan heard the front door shut and glanced out the window in time to see Jill climb into the car. *Solved that mystery*, he thought. *Wonder what she was doing here.* He took a bite of his sandwich.

"What are you eating?"

First words in over a week. Ryan held his breath and turned. He hadn't heard her come in, but she stood just inside the office door, wearing black yoga pants and a loose, red sweatshirt that said 'Art is whatever you choose to frame.'

"Hi," he said.

She took a few steps and wrinkled her nose at his sandwich. "Do you want some real food?"

He nodded slowly. "Yes, please."

She grabbed his plate, and he followed her into the kitchen. He stood by the door, watching as she moved around gathering ingredients, boiling water, slicing vegetables.

"I love you," he told her suddenly as she sautéed.

She glanced at him briefly and kept stirring, but said nothing. When she finished, she made a plate of bowtie pasta and tomato sauce with a small salad and brought it to the breakfast table. "Eat," she said.

He sat at the table, passing close to her and catching hints of lavender oil.

It was good. No, it was great. The best meal he could remember in a long while.

"We need to talk," she said.

Ryan nodded with his mouth full, trying to swallow.

"I'll start, you eat."

She sat across from him. Her red, tear-swollen eyes did nothing to detract from her beauty, and just the fact that she was so close made his chest ache.

"You hurt me. Bad. I don't…" Tears began to form at the corners of her eyes. "I don't know if I will ever be able to fully trust you again." She shook her head. "I don't know how I can trust you."

Ryan put his fork down and reached for her hands, but she pulled hers back.

"I love you, Ryan," she said.

His eyes filled with tears too.

"But I can't be with someone I can't trust. If this is going to work, we need to reset, figure this out, get back to where we were. We need to work the problems out together."

He nodded.

"And no more hiding things. We discuss everything."

He nodded again.

She wiped her eyes. "That's all I can handle for now." She stood, and he wanted to reach out to her, but instead remained still. She looked at him, then passed close by, touching his shoulder briefly, and left.

———————

Ryan cleaned up the kitchen. His hunger had fled with Karisa, so he put the pasta in a plastic container in the fridge, then headed back to his office.

He froze in the doorway after catching sight of Karisa looking through the statements on the desk. "Is it really bad?" she asked.

He sighed, walked to the desk, and opened his notebook. "It's not good. John told us to look over everything, make some decisions about what we don't need."

She crossed her arms and looked up at him. "What do you think?"

He shrugged. "Not sure, really. Selling the boat is probably top of the list."

She snorted.

"What?"

"I told you we never should have bought it in the first place."

Ryan's face turned red and he bit his tongue. He could see John right now, telling him to breathe. It was true, she had told him that. And they hadn't really used it but a few times in the last three years. It had seemed like a good idea for family time after his last promotion. "Yes, you did, babe," he told her. "You were right."

She looked at him in a strange way.

"The boat is just a drain on our resources, and we barely even use it. Also, we could trade in my car for a used one. Maybe even one with no payments."

"My car, too?" Karisa asked, quietly.

Ryan smiled slightly. "Let's start with just mine and see if the numbers add up. My goal is to be able to make all our payments with a little extra to build back our savings. John also said we could probably cut twenty percent of our expenses."

She laughed out loud, and Ryan chuckled too.

"Did you ask him if he wanted to see you walk on water while you're at it?"

Ryan smiled. "I told him I doubt we could do that."

"Doubt? Did you tell him it was impossible?"

"I think I did use those words actually, but I've been looking at some of what we're spending money on, and there are some places we can probably cut down."

She looked at the notebook.

"You've got to be kidding, we're going to cut down on food?"

"Well, we could cook more, that's supposed to be cheaper."

"We? You mean *me*."

"I could help more."

"Really? When has that ever happened?"

"Well—okay, you're right, I don't help much now, but I can try."

Ryan looked at the list again. "And this Hobby Lobby bill, do you know what that is?"

"My Etsy business," she said with her arms crossed again, eyes glaring. "You know, the one that made $2,000 last month."

He paused. "Well, it doesn't make sense to cut that, especially if you're earning more money than you're spending." He circled the expense. "Is that why Jill was here?" he asked, not looking up.

She moved to the window and looked into the night, then turned and leaned against the wall. "I've been talking with Jill for the last couple of weeks. She's been helping me with my business."

"Sounds like it's going well."

Another small smile. "It's good, really good actually," she said quietly. She nodded to the desk. "What are you going to do after you cut some of these things?"

"First of all, babe, *we're* going to cut things, because we're a team. We'll only cut what we agree on."

Ryan saw her smile slightly.

"Actions speak louder than words," she said. "But I appreciate your change of attitude. So, what are we going to do after *we* cut *our* expenses?"

"I think he's going to tell us how to invest it."

"Ryan, listen to me. We don't have money to invest. Does he know about investing? I don't think we're in a position to take risks"

"Well, he said he has mentored people before, and he and Jill invest in real estate."

"Just promise me that you won't make any financial decisions without me." She came back to the desk and firmly grabbed his chin. "I mean it. Promise me. This is the only way we get back our trust."

He looked into her eyes. "I promise."

She didn't smile. "Good." She looked down at his notebook. "So what else did our new financial advisor say?"

Ryan turned the page. "He wanted me to put down my strengths and weaknesses, and he said you could help. This is what I have so far."

He pointed at the notebook where he had written:

Strengths

Strategic thinking/a good coder

Good with numbers

A drive to get better

Weaknesses

Bad with money and investing

Not very lucky

Lack of self-discipline (I'm fat)

Procrastination

She considered the list. "You forgot to add 'butthead' under weaknesses."

He paused, then wrote that and looked back at her. "If we're going to be honest, let's do it right."

Now, she did smile. "And you forget some of your strengths," she said softly.

"What's that?"

"You're an all-around good guy—good husband, father, friend."

Ryan wrote that down. "And I'm funny," he added.

"Not as funny as you think."

"Ha, ha."

"See. And another weakness."

He looked at her, expecting another joke.

"Sometimes you just check out on me. You're not present."

He felt the emotion in her voice. "I'm sorry, babe." Ryan wanted to wrap his arms around her.

"Is that it?" she asked. "Did we finish your homework?"

Ryan turned the page. "Just one more thing. Where do we see ourselves in three years?"

She patted her belly. "A baby."

"Regardless if we have to trade your car in, we need a big car," he said.

She nodded. "It would be nice to get my business out of the garage."

He hadn't considered that before. "Do we need to start looking for office space?"

She put a warm hand on his shoulder. "It's still a bit early for that."

"Okay, well let me know, I'll start looking. I'd classify your business as one of our biggest assets now, and part of our future."

She put a hand on his other shoulder and Ryan could feel the warmth of her body against his back.

"So, we have no more debt, some savings in the bank, and a thriving business," Ryan said.

"A healthy baby," Karisa continued. "A bigger car and you're more present, spending more time with me and the kids, less stressed about work and bills."

"That's the dream, right?" he said.

CHAPTER
TEN

"Hello?" Ryan answered his cell. "Yes, it's in great shape. Lots of room for that, for sure. Why am I selling the boat? My wife is pregnant and I need to save money for another college fund. Sure, we can meet tonight, six o'clock, at the marina. I'll text you when I get there." Ryan hung up.

An inexplicable sadness filled him. They'd only ever used the dang thing a handful of times. The idea was prettier than the reality. It took a lot of coordination to get it off the dry dock and then weave through all the summer traffic to a semi-peaceful place on the ocean. He couldn't deny that the whole process took more effort than it was worth. This was the right thing to do.

Ryan saw Howard come out of the conference room, make eye contact, and then nod toward the elevator. Ryan met him as Howard pushed the down button.

"I'm starving, let's grab something to eat."

Penny's Bistro had been Ryan's main source of nutrition for most of his career at CaptivSoft, serving a selection of deli sandwiches, chips, and fountain drinks.

Howard stepped into line. "What do you want? I'm buying."

"I'm good, I brought my own today." Ryan had a big salad upstairs in the break room fridge. Every little bit of savings counted if they wanted to start investing this year. Also, since he'd begun hitting John's gym in the morning, he was feeling more fit, and healthy meals seemed to make sense all of a sudden.

"Don't be ridiculous, I told you I'm buying."

"Really, I have food upstairs. Just some water is fine. Thanks."

Howard shrugged. "Suit yourself." There were two more customers in front of him.

"I'll get us a table," said Ryan, moving through the half-filled restaurant. He chose a booth and Howard joined him a few minutes later, sucking on a straw from a large soda.

"So, I need you to come in this weekend, we got another big contract coming up." He handed Ryan a bottle of water and took another long sip. "I know it's last minute, but I need you to manage the coders on this one, just like last time."

"I've worked the last three weekends straight. I'm not going to be able to keep this up after Karisa has the baby, she's going to need help."

"Can't her mother fly in to help out? My mother-in-law basically lived in my house for three years when my two kids were born."

Howard's name was called and he went to pick up his meal.

Ryan was getting a little angry. Karisa's mom was planning on coming when the due date was closer, but that was beside the point. It was his responsibility. Howard was going to have to understand that his priority during that time was going to be his family.

Howard returned and began to unwrap his sandwich.

"Look, I have no problem coming in this weekend, but I just want to be clear that after this I really need to start spending more time with my family, more regular hours and weekends off."

Howard swallowed, then wiped his mouth with a napkin.

"Ryan, let's make this one a home run and I'll work with you on a schedule. We should be able to do a lot of this remotely. Will you be able to work from home on the weekends?"

"I think I can do that." Not ideal, but a good start.

"Fine. Also, next time I'm bringing you to Patterson's briefing. You need to get used to it anyway once you get promoted, and since you're the de facto chief coder now, you might as well get used to the heat."

"Okay by me."

Howard finished the rest of his lunch in silence while Ryan sipped on his water. It was weird, but he couldn't stop thinking about time. That word seemed to come out of John's mouth a lot: *if something provides you money, time, health, or happiness, it's an asset, but if something costs you money, time, health, or happiness it's a liability.* Right now, his job appeared to fall into the latter category. Ryan smiled. Obviously, John couldn't be talking about his job, though it did seem to fit the bill— it was taking time away from his family when they needed him the most and it wasn't making either Karisa or him happy at the moment.

When Ryan got home, he started crunching numbers in the notebook.

The guy was really interested in the boat—he didn't even haggle over the price. They would work out the details on Sunday.

He listed a few websites he'd heard offered freelance jobs. He'd need to do some research, but maybe he could work a side gig, make some of the money he lost back, and show Karisa how sorry he really was.

He heard a light knock and turned. Karisa was at the door dressed in one of Ryan's T-shirts.

"Hey, babe," said Ryan. "Stealing my clothes now?"

Karisa gave him a sheepish grin. "My pajamas—most of my wardrobe actually—are starting to get snug. I'm going to have to go shopping for some maternity clothes soon. You look deep in thought. What are you doing?"

"Just going through the expenses to see what else I can cut. I think I found a buyer for the boat."

"Someone bought that floating money pit?"

That hurt, despite its accuracy, but Ryan took it graciously. "The guy seemed really interested."

"Well, that's really good news. What else did you decide to cut?"

Ryan tapped his Grow notebook. "I only cut things that directly affected me so far. No more Starbucks, fast food, work lunches. I've been taking my lunch and filling up my water bottle at the water fountain at work. I wanted to get your thoughts on the rest."

She came over and put her arm casually around his shoulder as she looked at his notebook.

"Can we cut any of these streaming services?"

Karisa laughed. "I barely watch any television. We can get the kids together tomorrow and tell them we're cutting two of the services and let them choose."

"Good idea." Ryan circled all the streaming companies. He tapped the notebook with his pen. "How is the business doing?"

"Actually, I think this will be my best month. Jill had some really good marketing ideas, and I think I'll break about $4,000 profit this month."

"Wow!" He hugged her spontaneously, and she froze. He let his arm drop and continued. "That's really amazing, babe."

"I think I might need to hire someone, at least part-time," she said, ignoring the awkwardness of the moment.

Ryan nodded. "That makes sense. It would be good to have someone familiar with everything you're doing to hold down the fort for a little while when the baby comes." Ryan circled his car payment. "I'm going to see about trading in my BMW this weekend too, get a used car with no loan payments if possible."

"Really? You love that car."

He nodded. "Yep, but we just don't need it. Also, I spoke to Howard. I told him I needed to start a more regular schedule so I can help with the kids. I could also help with your business more as well."

He looked up at her when she didn't reply and saw the beautiful smile on her lips. She bent down and kissed his cheek. "That would be wonderful," she said.

If spending time at home meant seeing more of that smile, he was all in.

CHAPTER ELEVEN

"Are you *sure* we're not lost?" Karisa asked for the third time.

Part of Ryan wanted to be annoyed at her lack of faith in his navigation skills, but a bigger part had to admit that they were in the middle of nowhere and definitely heading away from civilization. The GPS showed they were only four minutes away, but it was starting to look like their destination was the Pacific Ocean. Shouldn't they have at least gotten to the neighborhood by now?

He decided to feign confidence. "Of course, we're almost there." Just as Karisa began to reply, he spotted a small structure down the road. "Look, there's something up ahead!" The relief in Ryan's voice was a rather embarrassing admission of his own doubt. When the GPS took them past the house and on toward the ocean, Ryan began to panic again, but then they passed a group of trees, and the GPS instructed him to turn just after a couple of houses that came into view on the left.

"See, we're here. No need to worry…" Ryan's voice trailed off as they turned into a long driveway leading down to a beautiful, modern building. The large home was all angles and glass, with garage doors big enough for fire trucks, and an infinity pool perched on the side of the mountain slope, just visible from the driveway. Ryan whistled softly as he got out of the car and closed his door, walking to the front of the vehicle to reach for Karisa's hand. "Still worried about whether or not they can give us good financial advice?" Ryan teased as they walked past the artfully arranged landscaping to the front door.

"Worried? Heck, now I'm just hoping they'll write us a whole book explaining how they achieved this! Do you really think we could get here? I mean, obviously, John and Jill know what they're doing, but this—this is so much more than I could ever imagine us having."

Ryan nodded his agreement as they approached the front entrance. Jill's smiling face was visible through the glass door before she opened it to greet them. "Welcome, we're so glad you could make it. Did you find the place okay?"

"Oh, sure, it was no trouble at all," Ryan replied, ignoring Karisa's look.

"Your home is lovely." Karisa's tone was awestruck as she took in the pale hardwood floors, entire walls of glass, and breathtaking ocean views.

"Thank you, we love living here." Jill led them to a pristine white sofa. "John's just finishing up. Can I get you a glass of wine, Ryan? And Karisa, what would you and the baby like?"

"Maybe just some water for now," said Karisa.

Ryan agreed, and Jill headed over to the long kitchen island.

"Can you believe this place?" Ryan asked.

Karisa snorted quietly. "I don't care what advice they give us, our house will never be this clean, and we could never get away with white couches." Ryan chuckled softly, grateful that they seemed to be able to banter playfully once again.

John entered from the patio. "We meet again," he said, immediately giving Karisa and Ryan each a hug. "How's the baby treating you?"

Karisa ran an affectionate hand over her stomach. "Really good, thanks."

Jill returned with glasses full of ice water.

"John, thanks so much for all the help you've given us, we really appreciate it," said Karisa.

John waved his hand dismissively. "Don't worry about it. Like I told Ryan, Jill and I have had our challenges and found ourselves in a tough financial situation. If we hadn't had friends and mentors to help us through it, I don't know what we would have done."

Jill nodded. "We understand exactly how you feel. It's like the carpet was pulled from underneath you, and now you're trying to get back on your feet."

Karisa looked around the living room. "I don't mean to be rude, but it looks like you made a good comeback."

"It didn't come easy, that's for sure. We made some mistakes in the past with the stock market and our real estate investments," said John.

"Tell me about it," said Karisa, glancing at Ryan.

John patted Ryan on the back. "Don't misunderstand what we're saying, Karisa, our real estate investments are what helped us get what we have now. But in 2008, we were doing it all wrong. We thought we had it figured out, and we lost almost everything in the market crash. We had to reassess and learn from our mistakes, and while we did that, we were living pretty spartan-like."

"You can say that again," Jill said. "Remember when we house hacked two of our rooms out?"

"You did what?" asked Karisa in shock.

John laughed. "Yeah, there were some lean times. We turned the closets into little kitchens with a microwave and some cupboards, then we rented them out. We almost covered our monthly mortgage payment, though it was a little cramped until we got back on our feet."

"That's crazy!" said Karisa.

"When I say spartan, I really mean it. We went to the bare minimum just to save the money to invest again. No eating out for like a year. We even made it work with one car for a while. Every little bit helped."

"We made a friendly competition to see who could spend less during the week," said Jill.

"I don't know how friendly it was," quipped John.

"You're just jealous because I always won."

"Of course you did, dear. Anyway, it was worth it," said John. "We made a new plan and used the extra money to get back into the real estate market, but this time we did it the smart way."

John moved beside Jill and put one arm around her.

"It wasn't easy," said Jill. She looked at John and smiled. "We had to step back and really analyze what we were doing. That's another way we saved money—no fancy restaurants or concerts, we found creative ways to have date nights at home, and we spent our extra time reading about real estate. We wanted to figure out where we went wrong. Still, sometimes I'm amazed at our journey. I just feel so blessed."

John nodded. "We both do. And now I'm amazed at how hungry I am. Can you two give me a hand in the garden? We need a few things for the salad."

Jill collected their glasses. "You guys do that and I'll finish up here."

Karisa and Ryan followed John outside, past the pool beside which a table had been set, and into a vegetable garden. John picked up a basket at the entrance.

"Usual suspects," said John. "Ripe tomatoes, cucumbers, and a few onions. I'll dig for the carrots." They started filling the basket. "So, Karisa, Jill was telling me about your business."

Ryan's heart warmed as he watched his wife smile. "She's really awesome, John. She's only been doing it for about six months, and she's already making a profit."

"It's picking up, but the more I make, the more time it takes," said Karisa.

"That's the thing, right," said John. "Time is your enemy and your friend with everything you do in business. You need to spend more time to make more money when you're starting out, but you also have to balance time with the ones you love, or what is it all for?"

Karisa nodded. "Exactly. That's exactly what I've been wrestling with."

"It's great that you recognize that need for balance early on. So many business owners don't. It's awesome that your business is doing so well. Just remember that it will take more time in the beginning. You're just getting started, so you're in the planting phase."

Karisa placed some cucumbers in the basket. "Planting phase?"

"I've learned that there are three phases to making a business successful. Lots of people look for 'get rich quick' methods of building a business, but from my experience, they don't exist. The only viable and safe way to get rich is slowly, by building a solid foundation. Most people don't make a profit in their first year starting a business, and in that sense, you're beating the averages, Karisa." John checked the basket. "I think we're good, let's get these washed up."

They began walking back to the house.

"Planting?" prompted Karisa.

John smiled. "Planting. A lot of work goes into starting a business, just like when you're planting a seed. The seed has to grow down and take root before it can come up out of the soil. The same thing can be said about your business. You're solving problems and figuring out processes. It's a lot of work for little reward. You need to push through without seeing the fruit of your success, but with the excitement of the potential of your business."

"That describes exactly what Karisa is going through," said Ryan. "We looked over her accounts last week, and it seems like she goes three steps forward and then two steps back. But, I also think that there will only be so much time she can spend working on the business, especially after the baby comes. So, she may be reaching her max profits soon."

John set the basket beside a sink on the patio and began washing the vegetables. "I know everyone has different visions for their business. When I started my gyms, I felt I was working twenty-four hours a day keeping it afloat— sometimes it felt like twenty-eight hour days. But my goal wasn't to work all day, every day, even if the money was good. I built systems, hired the right people. That's the second phase. The planting phase you have to do yourself, you have to live and immerse yourself in the business in order to understand all the details. The next phase is cultivating."

Jill came out with steaming bowls in her hands and placed them in the center of the table. "Are you guys talking about Karisa's wall art business? She does such great work!"

Karisa blushed. "Can I help?" she asked.

"No, we're fine," Jill said, moving to John's side. She took a cutting board down from a rack above the sink and began slicing the vegetables that were already clean. "Just sit and relax." The couple made short work of the salad and sat down at the table.

"This looks wonderful," said Karisa, as they all filled their plates.

There was a brief moment of crunching, then Ryan asked, "You said something about cultivating?"

John nodded. "Right, so if you think about a plant, after the seed sprouts from the ground, it's extremely vulnerable and needs water, sun, fertilizer, and protection from bugs and blights. Sometimes you mess up, but you learn from your mistakes. You're encouraged because you see growth. This is similar to your new business. After the first year or so, you're still doing a lot of the work and investing time, but you've solved most of your big problems. Now, you understand where you can start to make systems and even hire help to make your business more efficient. That way, you can focus on the parts of the business that only you can do."

"Are you telling me the goal of building my business is to have other people work it for me, like at your gyms?" asked Karisa.

John shook his head and took a sip of water. "Your business is your business. You control it, and you can choose to take as big a part in it as you want. What I'm saying is, eventually, you might have other priorities and interests. I always looked at my businesses and investments as a means to an end. I wanted to live my life on my terms. And the only way to do that was to systemize everything I could, which is part of the final phase, harvesting. After your hard work has paid off, everything is dialed in and you have the right people and processes in place, your business doesn't take as much effort and you have more free time. For me, that was the goal."

"But sometimes," said Jill. "He needed to be reminded."

John laughed and looked at Karisa. "I know what it's like to build something from the ground up. It becomes a part of you. I get that. But Jill reminded me that it was a stepping stone to the life we dreamed of, which didn't include working insane hours or not spending time with our family."

Karisa thought about that while they continued eating.

"Ultimately," said Jill, "You just have to decide what you want."

———————————

After dinner and a sunset walk around the property, Ryan and Karisa said their goodbyes. They drove away in silence, both lost in their own thoughts. Karisa tapped on her phone for a bit, then put it down and looked up.

"The kids are fine. I told Maria we're heading home," she said. They traveled some without saying anything, then Karisa turned to him. "I want that."

"What, the house?" Ryan asked.

She laughed out loud. "Well, yeah. Who wouldn't? But I want that life for us. I want us to be together more, not worrying about bills, planning our lives together instead of reacting to life."

"I agree. How do we get there?"

Karisa held up her phone. "I googled house hacking. I think we should consider it."

"I don't know, having someone else living in our house? And you're pregnant on top of that."

"I know, but listen. The kids don't use the playroom much, hell they barely come out of their own rooms nowadays. It has its own bathroom and entrance from the backyard, we can just lock the door that connects to the rest of the house. Guests could come and go as they please. There are a bunch of examples online, it seems pretty simple. I know it's crazy, but if we rent it out for only fifteen days a month for $150 a night, that pays our mortgage, and everything else can go into savings."

Karisa had begun speaking faster and faster as she explained.

"We could use the extra money to hire some help for your business," said Ryan.

She shook her head. "It can wait. I'd rather build our savings back, and then start investing in the stock market."

"Not real estate?"

"Maybe later, but I don't think we have enough to start in real estate right now even if we wanted to."

Ryan remained quiet for a while after she finished, minding the road.

"What are you thinking?" she asked.

"I was just thinking…" he began, then stopped. "I really love you."

Now, she was quiet. "I love you too, Ryan." She paused as if in thought. "So, we're doing this?" she said finally.

"I wouldn't want to do it with anyone else."

"But slowly," she said. "We figure this house hacking thing out, and then how to invest slowly. No more crazy, impulsive risks. And we do it together."

Ryan reached for her hand and she didn't resist. "From now on, always together."

CHAPTER
TWELVE

Ryan turned on his work computer and took a few swallows from his water bottle as the system initiated. His phone vibrated. It was John calling. "Hey, John," he answered.

"Hey, Ryan. I'm leaving on a ski trip on Monday with Jill, so do you want to go mountain biking tomorrow?" asked John.

"Can't, sorry. I'm putting the final touches on our new Airbnb."

"That's awesome!" said John. "Okay, let's meet up in about three weeks after I get back. Can't wait to hear about how the room rental goes."

"Deal."

They worked out the times, then hung up.

Karisa and Ryan had spent the last two weeks making plans for the house hack, and this weekend they were going to put the final touches on the room and then list it on Airbnb. It was a little weird having a stranger basically living in their house, but exciting too. Finally, Ryan felt they were doing something proactive to make their future better.

"Ryan."

He turned to see Howard nodding toward the conference room.

"Patterson is calling a meeting. Let's go."

Ryan gave him a thumbs up and retrieved his notebook. When he arrived, the room was almost full, and he took a seat next to Howard. "What's this about?" he asked his boss.

"New client, I think."

Dave Patterson entered the room, and everyone immediately went quiet. "All right, we have a client briefing on Monday, a really big one." His administrative assistant came in and started handing out booklets. "Here's the profile. I'll need everyone in here tomorrow, 10 am sharp, to discuss strategies."

No one groaned, but Ryan could see some disappointment in their faces. *At least I'm not an executive yet*, he thought.

"Ryan, I want you to come up with a plan of action for your team. Howard will get you up to date on the requirements, but basically we need a good estimate of hours charged for the project, timelines, the usual."

Patterson moved on down the line of executives, giving out instructions.

Ryan wrote in his notebook, turned it to Howard, and tapped on it with his pen.

Howard looked down at the writing. *I can't come in tomorrow. Family stuff.* Howard looked up at Ryan.

Patterson had finished micro-managing. "All right, get to work everyone, and I'll see you tomorrow. I'll bring the donuts."

"Hey sir, Ryan and I need a word."

"Sure, one sec." Patterson spoke softly to his admin assistant who took a couple of notes, and by then the room was empty. He looked up "What's up?"

Ryan spoke. "Hey sir, I can do the numbers tonight, no problem, but I can't make the meeting tomorrow due to some family obligations."

Patterson stared at Ryan for a second. "I thought we spoke about this a few weeks ago. The only reason I'm giving this to you is because you are our pick for the junior management job."

"Dave, I can brief it tomorrow, it's no problem," said Howard.

Patterson's eyes never left Ryan's. "I know you can, Howard, you can probably do the whole job. That's not the point. Before we promote young Ryan here, we should probably make sure he's as dedicated as the rest of us. Well, are you, Ryan?"

Ryan glanced at Howard. "Sir, we'll be ready tomorrow, if Howard is willing to give the presentation for the coders. I can't make it, but I'm confident the information will stand on its own." Ryan kept Patterson's gaze.

"Okay, I guess we'll see." Patterson's voice was stoic. He stood up and walked out of the room.

―――――――――――――

That evening, Ryan helped Karisa clear the table and clean up the kitchen. Once they finished, he gave her a quick kiss then headed over to Michael's room.

"Are you doing okay, buddy?"

Michael sighed. "Math."

"Well, you know your old dad is a whiz at math."

"Really? Mom never seems to be able to help me."

Ryan walked over. "Well, Mom is more the artistic type. She's probably better at helping with your reports. But I'm your man for math. What are you working on?"

He spent the next hour walking Michael through the equations step by step until he was confident his son understood the formulas.

Standing to leave, Ryan ruffled Michael's hair. "Let me know if you have any more math problems, buddy."

"Thanks, dad. I think I actually get it now." The look of wonder on his face filled Ryan with a mixture of pride and shame. He was so glad to see his son succeed and feel more confident, but how much sooner could he have felt that way if Ryan was around more often to help with things like homework?

Ryan wandered down the hall to Joy's room, where he found his wife and daughter snuggled up in bed with a book. Joy read aloud while Karisa listened and followed along, interjecting to help sound out the occasional tough word. Ryan stood in the doorway listening and watching as a small smile played across his lips. When they were finished, he came into the room and kissed Joy goodnight.

Karisa walked out and Ryan shut off the light, then they walked arm in arm to the office.

"Patterson wanted me to work this weekend," he told Karisa.

"Unbelievable!"

"I told him I had family commitments."

"You did?" She looked at him in surprise and he smiled.

"I did. So, I have to work on the presentation and send it to Howard, but I don't have to go in. You're stuck with me tomorrow."

She hugged him. "Sounds like my perfect day."

CHAPTER THIRTEEN

R yan, Karisa, and the kids spent the morning buying supplies, though Ryan was still debating whether he had made the right decision not to go into work. He'd spent all night getting Howard the numbers, double and triple-checking his work.

"What's wrong?" Karisa asked as they drove home.

Ryan looked over at her quickly. "Hmm? Nothing's wrong."

"I know when you're in your head."

"Is that a superpower I don't know about?"

"You should, I've been using it on you for fifteen years."

"Fifteen? We've only been married for twelve."

She laughed. "Oh, honey, I've been in your head since the day we met."

Ryan chuckled at that.

"So? What's going on, spill it."

Ryan drove a few more blocks. "I'm just thinking about the promotion."

"What about it?"

"Well, I didn't go in today to attend the big planning meeting, and I don't know how that will affect their decision to promote me."

"Hun, are you the best at what you do?"

He smiled. "I am."

"Then, they would be stupid not to promote you. It's in their best interests to promote the best. If you don't get the promotion because of this weekend, then they were never going to give it to you in the first place. So screw 'em."

Ryan cocked his head and glanced at her again. "How'd you get so smart, Karisa Elaine Brooks?"

"I've been this way awhile," she answered with a wink. "Did you just notice?"

He reached over and took her hand. "Nah, I always knew I married up."

When they arrived at home, they unpacked the car together, then began setting up their new rental room. Ryan laid down drop cloths and began touch-up painting while Karisa arranged some generic framed pictures of landscapes they had picked up at a second-hand store. Michael and Joy even helped move the things out of the playroom into the garage, reminiscing over unused toys.

"Hey," Ryan called out to Michael, who had just finished hauling out the last of the toys. "Wanna help me put together this table?"

Michael sent his father a surprised look before nodding and heading over.

"Just hand me that screwdriver, then hold this leg in place, yeah, just like that. Perfect! I knew this would go faster with your help. We just need to do three more."

The grin that covered Michael's face tugged at Ryan's heart. "Hey, I didn't know you knew how to do this stuff, Dad."

"Honestly, there's not much to it, just follow the directions. Although, I do think my handyman skills have improved since that Habitat project."

"That's so cool! Do you think I could go next time?"

"I don't know, buddy. I'm not sure you're old enough, but if you want, we can definitely find somewhere to volunteer together."

"Yeah, that'd be cool," Michael mumbled shyly.

Once they'd finished setting up the table, Ryan unboxed and plugged in the new microwave, and Karisa set up plates and cutlery on the new table while Joy filled a small vase with flowers.

When they were finished, they stood in the middle of the room with their arms around each other and the kids.

"There's something missing," Ryan said.

Karisa looked around. "Looks perfect to me," she said. "And you said I got to make all the calls on decorations."

Ryan shook his head, stopped, then held up a finger. "I know." He reached under the bed and pulled out one of Karisa's original creations.

"Where did you…" said Karisa.

Ryan took down the generic art above the bed frame and replaced it, then backed up and put his arm around her again.

"There, now it's perfect," Ryan said, then turned to kiss Karisa on the cheek, but she turned as well and their lips met.

"Did someone say ice cream?" Michael asked.

Everyone laughed.

———————————

Later that night in their bedroom, Ryan posted the photos on Airbnb.

"Do you want to do the honors?" he asked

Karisa reached over and pushed return, then laid her head on his shoulder.

"And now, we are officially house hackers," said Ryan.

"How long do you think it will take for us to get our first…"

The computer dinged.

Ryan moved the mouse, hovered over parts of the webpage, then clicked twice. "We have our first guest, next weekend."

"You're kidding!" Karisa looked at the screen. "You're pulling my leg—one of your friends signed up."

"No, I'm not. It says right here, George reserved three nights. He'll be arriving on Friday."

"We should stock the fridge with a couple of things to make him feel welcome."

Ryan laughed. "He's not our house guest."

Karisa shook her head. "I read that if you leave extras, you get higher ratings and that helps to get more bookings."

"Where did you read that?"

"A book I found on Amazon."

He tickled her and she screamed.

"What else have you been reading about?"

"A lot of things," she said, still giggling a little. "I read about investing in stocks and bonds. That sounds like something we should do with our money, and talk to a financial advisor."

"And real estate."

She pursed her lips. "It just seems so complicated. I read one book, but there seem to be so many options and rules and loopholes. I'm just not comfortable putting our money there. There are so many unknowns."

Ryan nodded. "Fair enough. I'm not sure I understand it all yet, either."

"Clearly not."

He nodded. "Also fair. I read a couple more books about it last week though. Let's not rule it out just because I'm an idiot. I mean, John and Jill said they made their money that way."

"And lost it."

"Right, but not in that order."

She smiled. "I'm willing to keep an open mind, but I just want to learn about all the options. So, if you agree to keep an open mind about other options, I'll still consider real estate."

He held her face and kissed her.

"What was that for?" she asked playfully.

"Just sealing our deal with a kiss," he said, stroking her cheek. "And keeping my options open."

CHAPTER FOURTEEN

Three weeks later, John texted Ryan for another adventure. *Let's meet at the pier...and prepare to get wet.*

Ryan saw the boards in the back of John's truck as he pulled up. "Are we surfing?" he asked as John stepped out.

"Paddleboards. We're going to have a board meeting."

Ryan laughed as he helped unload.

"So, how's everything going?" asked John, as they walked to the beach.

"House hacking is working really well. We've had twelve days rented over the last three weeks, seven five-star reviews."

"That's great."

Ryan nodded. "We sold the boat. We didn't make much, but at least we're not paying the loan and dry dock fees anymore. I also traded in my car, so no more car payment. Plus, we combined our credit cards into a new one with no interest for a year. And we started a strict spending and savings plan. Karisa got on board—she's been really good at this."

"How do you feel?"

"Good. I feel really good. I have to talk it over with Karisa, but we might be ready to do some small investments in three to four months."

"I'm so happy for you guys," John said. He walked into the surf, put his board into the ocean, stepped on, then paddled into deeper water.

"You make it look easy," said Ryan, standing knee-high in the cool water, stalling as the waves lapped around him.

"Don't worry," John laughed. "It just takes a little balance, like most of life. And the fall is a soft landing, which life doesn't always give you."

Ryan stepped on his board, wobbling to get his balance, then paddled carefully toward John.

A small wave hit them. John rode it like a pro, but Ryan toppled into the water.

"I might not be cut out for this," sputtered Ryan. "And that's not my Gremlin speaking, that's just an honest assessment of how wet I am. Any advice on how to stay on the board?"

"Find your equilibrium," John maintained his distance as Ryan struggled to get back on the board.

"Well duh, Yoda. You're not going to compare this to life again, are you?" asked Ryan.

John smiled. "I might, especially if you fall off again."

"Which I'd rather not."

"Okay, stand up slowly and feel the board beneath you. Focus on the ocean about twenty feet in front of your board and then roll with the water. Paddle into the waves and don't be rigid. It's all about being aware, staying present, and really paying attention to where you are and what's coming at you."

Ryan was standing again, tentatively paddling toward John.

They moved at a casual pace, with Ryan enjoying the warm sun on his skin and the salty breeze hitting his face. He didn't fall again, though he had a couple of close calls.

"Hey, John, Karisa and I have a few financial questions for you."

"Sure, what's on your mind."

"Karisa is concerned about investing in real estate after my mistake, and she has been reading some books about investing in stocks. She thinks we can get started sooner with less money down. Do you think that's the best way for us to go?"

They paddled for a few seconds before John replied. "Ryan, there are a bunch of ways to invest your money, and only you two can decide what you're most comfortable doing. I'll give you the best advice I can for whatever you choose to do, but let me tell you why I prefer rental real estate investing. In my experience, it provides the safest, fastest, and best way to financial freedom."

"I'm curious why you think that," Ryan said. "There seems to be so much more money on the line."

"It's true, the initial investment is more than some other methods," said John, paddling through a small wave and watching Ryan ride through it. "You're getting the hang of it now." John paddled some more. "But I also love that I don't have to spend all my time focusing on investments. Once I purchase a rental property, I have a team that supports me and helps manage the property. Plus, in the stock market, you can definitely make money, but you have to constantly buy and sell stocks in order to earn a decent income. Real estate isn't a totally passive activity either, but it doesn't require the constant attention of the stock market to be successful."

"So, you only buy rental properties? Doesn't flipping houses make money faster?"

"The way I invest is actually kind of boring compared to the overnight success stories of people flipping houses, trading in the stock market, or cryptocurrency. I invest in stocks too, but it's too unpredictable and unreliable for me to make it my primary wealth-building strategy. Stocks can change direction in an instant. Real estate is a slower moving investment where I can see the trends and adjust my plans if needed."

"I guess that makes sense," Ryan said.

John started to turn around, making a wide turn until they were heading back to their point of origin. "The way I invest is low in drama and stress. I invest for the long-term because I believe that slow and steady wins the race. When the market collapsed in 2008, I learned that investing based on the belief that the price of the property will increase over time is an approach grounded in hope, not logic. However, owning properties that generate consistent cash flow every month is much less affected by real estate values dropping. You get about the same amount of cash flow whether the market is expanding or contracting. That cash flow is your lifeblood to financial freedom because it usually comes consistently, like a paycheck."

"But what about vacancies? I don't want to have a mortgage on an investment property that I can't get rented."

"Real estate goes up and down just like most markets, but the demand for rental properties will always be there. People will always need a place to live, and the last time I checked, people prefer to live indoors." John winked. "As long as you do your research and make sure to buy a property with positive cash flow from day one, you should be fine."

They were quiet for a time, the only sound coming from the calm ocean and the small splashes of the paddles. Ryan felt a lot more confident on the board now and wasn't afraid of falling into the water again. What John had said made sense, but he knew that he and Karisa had a lot of learning to do.

———————

Ryan helped John load up the truck.

"John, you're always so relaxed, and I'm standing here with my mind moving a thousand miles a minute. You'll probably tell me something like, 'it's all about balance' or 'just breathe,' right?"

John laughed out loud. "Let me show you something. I think it's time to talk about your future self."

"Like when you asked me to picture myself in three years?"

"Something like that, but I want you to go deeper now. Lie down, face up on the beach." Ryan lay on the warm sand as John continued talking. "I'm going to walk you through this exercise to meet your future self."

"Time travel, I like it. Maybe I can make some money, like in *Back to the Future*."

"Good movie," said John, "but making money in the real world is done through good habits, not trying to game the system. People don't decide their futures. They decide their habits, and their habits decide their futures."

"More Gandi?" Ryan asked.

"An Australian actor named Fred Alexander, actually. Basically, if you make small incremental changes every day, you can make large changes in yourself. But, the question is, what changes? If you don't know the end state, how do you know how to get there? This exercise will help you find your goals. Ready?"

"Ready."

"Okay, this might be a little California Woo Woo at first, but bear with me, it will be worth it by the end."

"Let's do it."

"Get grounded. One of the best ways to get grounded is to close your eyes and take a deep breath in, deep deep deep, feel your rib cage expand, breathe that breath in really deep, hold it for a moment and let it go. Then take another deep breath in, really noticing the breath filling your lungs, and then let it go. Take a couple more deep deep breaths, and allow yourself to become more relaxed, and more comfortable."

Ryan let his body relax, but his mind was racing. What exactly were they doing?

"I'm going to invite you to take a little mental journey. And in this mental journey, I'm going to be asking you some questions. I'll give you the questions after, to help you remember them, so don't focus on that, just focus on the now. As you get more relaxed, more grounded, more comfortable, I want you to imagine that spot between your eyes, and imagine there's a light between your eyes. Notice the color of this light."

Ryan sensed a green light appearing between his eyes.

"Now imagine that light becoming a beam, a beam of light that extends from right between your eyes, out, toward space. Imagine following that beam of light up, into space, following the beam of light up, away from the world, moving further and further away from the earth, moving through the clouds, moving higher and higher up this beam of light through space, feeling the darkness and the peacefulness of space. Seeing the earth below you get smaller and smaller. And as you move further and further out into space, imagine that you look up ahead and you see another beam of light, a different color from the one that you followed out into space. And that beam of light is intersecting with the beam of light that you're following."

Ryan saw his green beam intersect with a yellow beam.

"Now imagine following that other beam of light back toward earth. Moving along that beam of light, moving toward earth. Getting closer and closer to the big ball of blue and green with white clouds wisping around it. And you realize that this beam of light is moving you back toward earth ten years in your future. You're about to get the experience of seeing your life ten years in the future. As you move down this beam of light, getting closer and closer to earth, notice where the beam of light intersects with the earth. Make your way down the beam of light, landing upon earth, and notice where you are. And as you look up ahead, you see a dwelling. This is the home of your future self. This is where you live ten years in the future. Notice this place, the home of your future self. Notice what it looks like. Notice if there are trees or flowers."

Ryan stood before a two-story house, bigger than the one they lived in now, but not huge. He could smell a combination of flowers from the front garden. The yard was definitely bigger than his current house. He wouldn't want to have to mow all that grass. Then, he saw an electric robot lawn mower appear from around the corner of the backyard. *Cool*, he thought.

"Make your way toward the front door of this home, and ring the doorbell and realize that on the other side of this door is your future self. It's you, ten years in the future. As the door opens, notice this person, your future self. Notice how your future self welcomes you in and greets you. Notice what your future self looks like. Notice what he is wearing. Get a feeling of this person."

The face of Ryan's future self was a bit more lined than the one he was used to seeing in the mirror every day, but he was so much thinner and more fit that he didn't actually look any older. Or maybe it was the relaxed, carefree air he had about him that made him look so young. In this future, Ryan wasn't tired from the office or stressed about money. He wore swim trunks and a T-shirt with a pair of flip flops and an easy smile.

"Your future self invites you to come inside. As you walk inside this home, look around. Take in this home of your future self. Are there photographs? Notice the colors and the feeling of this place."

Ryan walked into the beautiful, comfortable home, noticing the entire wall going up the stairs was covered in Karisa's moss art. *Nice to know she didn't leave my future self for being a workaholic*, Ryan thought wryly. As he looked around, he noticed a beautiful family portrait above the mantle with older versions of Michael and Joy, as well as another little girl he didn't recognize.

"Your future self invites you to come in and sit down for a comfortable conversation. As you sit down with your future self, you probably have some questions you would like to ask. Begin with this question: future self, in the last ten years, what stands out most in your memory? And listen to what your future self has to tell you. And now, ask your future self, what do I need to do to get from where I am to where you are? What would be helpful for me to know to get to where you are? Listen to your future self's reply."

Ryan's future self sat at his desk, in front of a collage of twenty different framed photos of houses and apartments, and talked about his journey, telling him the most important change was the little things every day. Every decision had a consequence.

"And now, there are probably other questions you would like to ask your future self," Ryan heard John say. "Go ahead and take some time to ask any questions that you might have."

Ryan looked at his future self: confident, not stressed, happy.

"Did we get the junior management promotion? Did we make senior manager?"

Future Ryan shook his head. "We made some hard choices, but it turned out alright. We made our own way," he said.

Our own way? Ryan wondered what that meant. "Who's the little girl I saw back in the living room, in that family portrait above the fireplace?" Ryan asked his future self.

A warm smile filled Future-Ryan's face as he replied. "That's your daughter. Her name is Hope."

"It's time to go now," John's voice interrupted. "But you realize you can come back to this place any time. Your future self will always be here to be a wise mentor or guide. As you make your way back to the door with your future self, do whatever you want to do to say goodbye. Make your way through the door and back into the front of the home and as you look up ahead, notice that beam of light that brought you here ten years into the future, and imagine following that beam of light back up toward space, moving further and further up the beam of light, deeper and deeper into space, looking up ahead and seeing the other beam of light that took you into space originally. Follow that beam of light back toward earth, moving back, closer and closer to the earth, realizing that you're coming back to the present, moving further and further down the beam, seeing the ocean and arriving back on the beach, wiggling your fingers and toes, becoming more aware, taking a deep deep breath in, and when you're ready, open up your eyes."

Ryan felt the sand beneath him and heard the soft lapping of the ocean waves. He opened his eyes, wiping away a tear.

John helped him to his feet "How do you feel?"

"I feel good. I feel focused."

"That's good. Now, go through your days and do things your future self would thank you for." John paused. "Why are you smiling? What did you see?"

———————————

Ryan drove home with his mind on fire. He wanted to start investing now, he wanted to get to his future life as fast as possible. Relaxing. Not stressing or worried about last-minute work projects. And that robot lawn mower was cool, he'd never seen one before, but he'd read about them in a magazine.

He wanted to talk to Karisa about their future selves; he wanted to get started now.

His cell rang. He saw Michael's name pop up on the car display and answered the phone.

"Hey, Michael. Everything okay?"

"It's mom." Ryan realized he was crying.

"What's wrong?"

"The ambulance took her away."

CHAPTER
FIFTEEN

"Placenta previa," the doctor said.

He hadn't even heard those words uttered together until he'd entered Karisa's hospital room that Saturday afternoon, his heart in his throat. He saw her in the bed, covered in sterile white sheets, looking pale and fragile with cables and tubes coming out of her.

Then, Ryan vaguely remembered the words 'stable', 'bed rest', and 'less active', as he followed her wheelchair to the exit with the kids in tow.

He spent the weekend attempting to restore the household to normal, getting the kids to their events, making sure Karisa was comfortable and wanted for nothing. She slept most of the time and told him that she felt fine, but in his mind, at his core, he couldn't help but think that he had almost lost her.

He called Howard and told him he'd be a little late, then he got the kids off to school, and she forced him out the door.

"I'm fine. I'll be fine. Go to work." So, he went, driving in a trance, his thoughts never far from her.

Howard saw him come in and told Ryan to have a seat in his office and he'd be there in five minutes. *Probably another client,* Ryan thought absently.

"Congratulations!"

Ryan spun around, startled because Howard had almost shouted the word as he walked into the office.

"You got it!" Howard approached him with his hand outstretched and Ryan rose to his feet in a daze.

"What are we talking about?" asked Ryan.

"The promotion! It's yours. Patterson was a bit of a hard ass, but even he couldn't deny your results. You're our new Junior Manager of Coders."

"I… " Ryan didn't know what to say, didn't know how he felt. Five years ago he never would have expected to be having this conversation. Then, from the moment Howard had mentioned it four months ago, it was always on his mind, managing his actions and how they would appear in the eyes of management. But now? Now, he just wanted to be home with the woman he loved more than anything. "I... Can I think about it?"

Howard stopped shaking his hand. "Think about it? What's there to think about?"

Ryan sighed deeply. "Karisa was in the hospital this weekend."

"Oh my God, is she alright? What happened?"

"She's... She's alright. Some complications with the pregnancy, but she's home on bed rest right now." *Alone. She's home alone right now.*

"Do you need anything? What can I do to help?"

Ryan shook his head. "No, thanks, Howard. She just needs to take it easy and stay off her feet more. In fact," he paused. He needed to be with her, help her. "I need to take a few days off to take care of my family."

"Of course, whatever you need. We'll talk about the promotion when you come back. Just call the admin and set up your time off. However much time you need."

Ryan shook Howard's hand again, with feeling. "Thanks, Howard. That means a lot."

———————

"What in the hell do you think you're doing?" Ryan asked as he entered the house to find Karisa at the sink washing dishes.

"Hey, hun."

"No, no, no. Go to bed. Now."

"I'm not helpless, and the kids left a mess after breakfast."

He grabbed her, turned her around slowly, took a towel, and dried her hands. "I got this."

"I'm not helpless," she said again, quietly.

"I know, but I got this. I took some days off work. I have some free time saved up for a rainy day." He kissed her hands. "This is as stormy as it gets." Wrapping his arm around her, he walked her back to their room, and she didn't resist.

After he got her settled in bed, he finished up the dishes. Michael had soccer practice, and it was Karisa's turn to drive a car full of kids home afterward in their parent carpool. Ryan picked up Joy at school and they watched Michael's practice as Joy did her homework, then Ryan made the rounds and they arrived home by 7 pm.

"Pizza?" asked Ryan, which was greeted by thunderous support. He placed the order, checked in with a sleeping

Karisa, then helped Michael with some more math until dinner arrived. It was 9 pm by the time he made it back to his room.

"Really?" Karisa asked when he walked out of the shower. "Pizza?"

Ryan shrugged.

"Did you save any for me at least?"

"I didn't, but there is delivery from your favorite restaurant."

"Jianluca's does delivery? That's amazing!"

"Well, no. I guess I meant your second favorite restaurant."

She grinned. "Forgiven."

He bent down to kiss her. "How are you feeling?"

"Tired."

"Promise me to take it easy, okay?"

She nodded.

"And let's put some ads out and hire someone to help you with the business."

"Already done."

"Babe, you need to rest."

"Please inform the activity police that I posted the ads before I went to the hospital. Not that I'd have to get out of bed to post some ads online… "

He sat next to her on the bed. "Okay, I'll let that pass."

She snuggled up beside him. "So, how did mentoring go before all the excitement happened?"

He put his arm around her. "It was really great. John had me do this future-self visualization exercise, which was kinda weird at first, but once I got into it, it was really cool."

"What did you visualize? What is your future self like?"

"Happy, relaxed. We had a ton of investment properties, lived in a bigger house, but I could tell I was working a lot less too. And I'd lost weight."

Karisa giggled at that. "All of that sounds wonderful."

He put his hand on her stomach. "And I saw this little girl."

Karisa moved closer into his side, her eyes beginning to drift shut. "We haven't talked about names yet," she murmured, her voice thick with fatigue. "I was thinking about Hope."

Ryan's mouth gaped open in shock, but by the time he'd gathered his wits enough to tell Karisa about the little girl from his future-self vision, she was sound asleep in his arms.

CHAPTER SIXTEEN

"Where are we going?" Karisa asked.

"It's a surprise. We're almost there, close your eyes." Ryan turned off the highway and quickly checked that her eyes were shut. She sat in the passenger seat, her cheeks a little flushed from excitement and a contagious grin on her face.

"Are we there yet?"

"Almost, keep them closed." Ryan turned down a street and then into a restaurant parking lot.

"I hope this isn't expensive, whatever it is." Her voice was suddenly serious.

"Don't worry about it," he said as he turned off the car.

"I'm serious, Ryan, we've been working really hard saving money, we don't need to splurge now."

"Open your eyes."

She did and looked right at him. "If this is expensive, you can drive right home and…" She turned her head and saw the sign. "Aw, hun…We can't afford this right now, let's go somewhere else."

"No way, it's your birthday and we're going to celebrate the right way because you deserve it. We've gone through a lot these last five months."

"How did you even get a reservation?" she asked, as he opened the door for her.

"Well." Ryan kissed her. "It seems we have really good friends."

"What does that mean?"

"It means," Karisa turned and saw John and Jill standing beside their truck, "that I know the owner," said John. "And he'll give us a birthday discount."

"Thanks, but you guys didn't have to do this."

"Forget about it," said Jill. "John's been promising to bring me back here for months, and this is as good an excuse as there gets." She gave Karisa a big hug. "How's the momma doing? John told me what happened, did the doctor give you a clean bill of health?"

They all started walking toward the entrance.

"We had a little scare, but I went back two weeks after the emergency room visit and he said it wasn't as serious as they thought at first. I just have to take it easy."

"I'm so glad you're okay," said Jill. "Does that mean you'll have to put the business on hold?"

Karisa looked at Ryan and smiled. "Well, we talked about it. We decided that even if we just keep the business where it's at, that's a win for us. Ryan took the last three weeks off and we hired an assistant for me, so now I mostly do the creative work without the heavy lifting."

"Good for you guys," said John. "But don't overdo it. Remember, if you haven't got your health, you haven't got anything."

"I don't think there is any danger of me overdoing anything," she kissed Ryan on the cheek. "Not with mother hen here."

The restaurant was crowded and busy inside. John spoke with the greeter, and they were led to a quiet table in the back.

"Are you guys still house hacking?" asked Jill.

"Oh yeah, it's turned into a great income stream. Thanks so much for the idea. It wasn't even that hard to do."

"I'm glad it worked out for you."

"It worked so well, we're about ready to start investing in our future. We're just trying to figure out the best way," said Ryan. "John, we've learned a lot through the books and other resources you told us about, but you once mentioned how there were five ways you can profit in real estate investing. What did you mean by that?"

John took a sip of water. "There are a lot of ways to profit from real estate investing, but I think I said there are five ways to profit from rental properties."

Karisa wrinkled her nose.

"What's wrong, Karisa, you don't like rental properties?" asked John.

"It's just, I've been learning a lot over the last months, and all of it seems to have a level of risk, but real estate seems to have the most risk because of the amount of money you need to invest in order to initially buy property. It just seems like you have a lot of eggs in one basket."

John nodded, then picked up the bottle of wine and filled Jill and Ryan's glasses, then his own. "You've learned the most important lesson, Karisa. As you said, there is some risk in all investments. So many people don't understand that. Still, in my opinion…"

"And mine," said Jill, clinking John's glass.

They laughed. "In our opinion," John continued, "investing in rental properties is one of the least risky options, and I'll tell you why." John ticked off a finger. "One, and what I consider the most important, monthly cash flow."

"Like a salary?" asked Ryan.

"Exactly. Basically, it's the money you put in your bank account each month after all the expenses for your rental properties are paid."

"See," said Karisa. "That's what I'm talking about, it seems like a big gamble that your expenses won't exceed your profits every month. How can you know ahead of time that it will be rented and you won't be stuck paying the mortgage out of pocket? "

"That's a good question," said Jill. "And the truth is that there are a lot of properties that won't produce positive monthly cash flow, especially here in southern California."

"Right," said John. "You have to do your research, analyze the numbers for the location where you want to purchase properties. You only invest in locations where rental statistics are high, so there is less probability of having an empty property. Then, you figure out the expenses on the property which include all the costs related to buying it, and the amount of rental income you can receive. If the income exceeds the expenses, you should be generating positive monthly cash flow, which is the goal."

"It still sounds risky," said Karisa.

John nodded. "We've already said there's risk in everything, but if you own a rental property with cash flow, waiting a couple months to find the best tenant will be well worth it down the line. Let's compare this to stocks. In order to really make money in the stock market you have to either be an expert or hire an expert you trust, and even then, you don't actually see any real income until you sell the stock. You can make dividends, but they aren't anything close to the cash flow you can make from rentals."

Karisa thought about that for a second. "That's a good point."

John finished his glass of wine, then topped off his glass and everyone else's. "And that leads us to appreciation."

"Didn't you mention that trusting on property appreciation was where you got in trouble before?" asked Karisa.

"That's right, you should never depend on appreciation alone when deciding on a rental property. However, the average annual property appreciation in the U.S. is about five percent over the last twenty years, though some markets are more than double that. In general, housing prices increase over time. I like to think of it as a 'free gift', though saying that out loud sounds a bit redundant since I've never heard of a gift you had to pay for. It's just a benefit you can probably expect if you choose this route of investing. Of course, in order to receive the actual cash profit from appreciation, you either need to refinance your property, take out a home equity line of credit, or sell the property."

"John!" A large man in a chef's hat approached the table bringing the enticing aroma of garlic and oregano with him. John stood as they hugged.

"Jianluca, how are you old friend?"

"I am better for seeing you. You need to come more often."

"That's what I've been telling him, too," said Jill, standing.

"Jill!" Jianluca also gave her a hug that lifted her from the ground.

"And these are our friends, Karisa and Ryan," said John.

Jianluca put his hands over his heart. "Any friend of John's is a friend of mine. Welcome to La Trattoria di Jianluca. Have you been here before?"

Karisa nodded, blushing. "This was our first date, but we haven't been able to come back because you're always booked."

"No, no, no. This won't do. Tonight, I make you all something special." He began to list off multiple dishes with ingredients that made Ryan's mouth water.

"Um, that sounds so wonderful, Jianluca. But would you mind leaving out the asparagus please?" She patted her belly. "The baby doesn't like it as much as I do."

"Mama mia, congratulazioni! Congratulations! Of course, no asparagus. Please, mi scusi, I will start cooking right now." He shook John's hand and left them.

"How do you know Jianluca?" asked Ryan.

"We've done a few deals together. Actually, we own this building together."

"Really?"

"Yeah. I started in single family properties, but I eventually expanded to commercial, multi-family, mobile home parks, and even self-storage. I've partnered with people from all walks of life. We have a saying, 'Don't wait to buy real estate. Buy real estate and wait.' Which leads me to my second reason, appreciation."

"But you said appreciation isn't dependable."

John nodded. "Some people buy investment properties only for the potential appreciation. I don't recommend that because betting on appreciation is really only speculation, as Jill and I, and so many others, unfortunately, learned in the market crash in 2008. So, I always look at appreciation as the icing on the cake. The nice thing is that when appreciation does happen it can definitely boost your wealth up a few sizes."

"Alright, so the main reason is cash flow, and the icing is appreciation," said Karisa. "What's next?"

"Tax benefits."

"Like tax loopholes?" asked Ryan.

"I guess you could call it that, but the reality is the government encourages real estate investors because they provide housing for the ever-growing population who rent, which strengthens and stabilizes the economy. Now, I'm far from being a CPA, so you should definitely consult one about this, but Uncle Sam rewards rental property owners with numerous tax benefits."

A waiter wearing a stiffly pressed tuxedo arrived with three different dishes. The aroma of freshly cooked vegetables, cheese, meat, and fresh bread drew an audible sigh of appreciation from the group.

"Oh my, this looks delicious. I can't think of a better birthday meal!" Karisa's grin lit up her entire face.

"This is not your meal, madam. This is the appetizer," the waiter replied with a polite nod before turning to leave.

"I don't know if we'll have room to eat all the food Jianluca will send, but it will certainly be fun trying," said John.

Everyone began to fill their plates as John continued. "Actually, I figured this out after my gym business grew to a few locations. I was shocked when my accountant told me how much in taxes I had to pay. Then, after I started investing in rental properties, I was pleasantly surprised to see those great tax benefits."

Talking ceased as everyone sampled each of the appetizers, and the soft Italian music playing in the background filled the silence.

"Jianluca has really outdone himself today," said John, looking at Jill. "We do need to come back more often."

Ryan agreed. The flavors were so much better than the take-out he'd brought Karisa a few weeks before.

"Amortization is the fourth way to generate wealth with rental properties," Jill continued as John added more food to his plate.

"Like paying a loan down?" asked Ryan with his mouth full, and he felt a light kick from Karisa under the table. "Sorry," he said, swallowing. "It's just so good."

"Exactly like paying a loan down," said Jill. "But it's not really *you* paying your loan down. Your tenants do that for you when they pay you rent money. Does that make sense? Your tenants are actually covering the cost of your mortgage—both the principal and the interest—each month, and as your mortgage gets paid, you gain more equity in the property even without appreciation. See why we count that as icing on the cake?"

"So, either through appreciation or amortization, you still gain equity in your property over time," said John. "Sometimes through both. Pretty cool huh?"

Both Ryan and Karisa nodded as they thought about all the information that was being thrown at them. Ryan mopped up the last of the sauce on his appetizer plate with a chunk of crusty bread and popped it into his mouth just as the waiter reappeared with entrees. Once the food had been distributed and everyone was once again eating, John continued to talk between bites.

"And the final way to make money is a little less known. Rental properties can be a hedge against inflation."

Ryan wiped his mouth with the soft linen napkin before speaking. "Like, it prevents inflation?"

"More like it protects you from inflation by making the assets more valuable. Let's say you buy a property next year with a mortgage. Over the next several years, inflation spikes. What happens to the dollar when inflation occurs?"

"The dollar is worth less as inflation goes up," said Ryan.

"Exactly. Let's say, then, ten years from now you are still paying your mortgage. The amount of the mortgage payment won't change over the life of the loan, but the amount of rent collected will most likely rise over time. See what I mean? Rental properties are one of the few investments that can actually benefit from inflation."

"John, I understand everything you're saying," said Karisa. "Even though real estate has all those benefits, stocks seem a lot easier. We wouldn't have to manage the tenants and fix plumbing and all of that."

"True, but there are companies that manage properties and take care of that for you," said John. "The management fees need to be rolled into the cost during your assessment, especially since your property might be located on the other side of the country."

Ryan and Karisa ate quietly for a few moments, lost in their own thoughts.

"One thing we haven't even mentioned yet is the use of leverage," continued John.

"What do you mean?" asked Ryan.

"Leverage is about using other people's money. I can't think of another investment where you can walk into a bank and say, 'Hey, I want to invest in something and I want you to pay for eighty percent of it.' In real estate, the bank becomes your partner. That says a lot about the trust financial institutions have in real estate."

"I'm not sure I completely follow you," said Ryan.

John put his fork down. "Let's say, for the sake of easy math, that you and I each have $100,000 to invest. If you use your money to buy stocks on margin, the value of those stocks is, say, $200,000. If I use my money as a twenty percent down payment to buy a rental property, then that property is valued at $500,000."

"I see where you are going with this," said Karisa. "But you still owe all that money to the bank."

"Correct, but bear with me. First of all, someone else is paying back your loan—your tenant. And if we jump forward fifteen years, assuming a five percent annual growth rate, let's look at the different scenarios. Your stock is worth about $415,000, which after you pay back the capital invested and the margin, is a $215,000 profit. You doubled your money in fifteen years, good job." John clinked his wine glass to Karisa's water glass.

Karisa nodded. "And your real estate?"

"Well, my property is now worth about $1,000,000 at the same growth rate as your stock. Plus, my original $400,000 loan has been paid down to about $260,000 by the tenants. So, if I sold the house I'd make a $740,000 profit."

Karisa's mouth fell open in shock. "That's more than seven times your investment!"

"More if you include the cash flow you'd make on the property for fifteen years plus all the tax deductions."

Karisa shook her head. "You make it sound easy John. What's the catch?"

"No catch. But it takes work and research and making decisions. Fortunately, there are people out there to help, property brokers to help you find the right market. Your job is to be smart and buy properties that bring a positive monthly income and have a good chance of appreciating in value. One of the big benefits of having five different ways to profit from rental properties is that if everything doesn't go perfectly with one of the ways to profit, you can still benefit from the other ways. Let the property managers do the day-to-day management so you can concentrate on your next property."

Ryan looked at Karisa. "What do you think?"

She rubbed her stomach. "I think the baby wants dessert."

———————

That evening, Ryan sat in his office writing in his Grow notebook.

Suddenly, two arms wrapped around him from behind, and Karisa nuzzled his neck. "It's late," she said softly. "What are you doing?"

He turned to face her. "Jotting down notes about rental real estate investments." He hugged her back. "I know we're not thinking of starting there, but I don't want to forget the stuff John said in case we decide to consider it in the future."

She stroked his hair, and they were quiet.

Ryan closed his eyes and listened to her breath, his head against her stomach. Then, he felt a soft punch, followed by another. "Hey, can you feel that?" he asked.

"Of course, silly. She's been boxing up a storm in there ever since we left the restaurant."

Ryan kept his cheek close.

"You know," Karisa continued, "I'd like to go ahead and do some more research on what John and Jill were talking about."

"Really? I thought you were focused on stocks."

"I know, but I think it's worth a look. John and Jill made a good case. I hadn't really been studying books on those types of investments, but I'll dig deep now."

"Me too. And we'll figure it out together." He felt another kick against the side of his face. *You too, Hope. Together means everyone.*

CHAPTER SEVENTEEN

"Is that all you're going to eat?" asked Howard.

They sat in Penny's Bistro. Howard had insisted on paying for lunch and Ryan had reluctantly accepted a salad.

"Yes, this is fine, thanks."

Howard wiped some mayonnaise from his mouth. "So, how is the wife doing? What did the doctors say?"

"Well, we had a scare, and basically she needs to rest and take it easy."

"That's good, right? Nothing too serious. I'm sure it will be fine."

Ryan nodded. "I really appreciate your support when I asked for all that time off. It really helped my family get settled into a good rhythm."

Howard waved a hand with his sandwich, losing a piece of lettuce. "Of course, of course. That's what I told Patterson—CaptivSoft is a family, and if we don't take care of our people, they can't take care of us." He put the sandwich down. "Speaking of which, that promotion is still yours. I explained the situation, and the firm delayed selecting a replacement until you came back. Are you ready to move into your new office?"

Ryan's gut twisted. After being at home for the last three weeks, he'd realized that he wasn't satisfied climbing the corporate ladder, that his priorities had changed. He wanted to spend more time with Karisa and the kids. He hadn't even realized that until last week, making lunch for the kids to take to school, when Joy had kissed him on the cheek and told him, "I like when you make lunch." Then, yesterday, Karisa hugged him tight and told him what he needed to hear. "Honestly, we'd like you home more, too. Just remember, CaptivSoft chose you because you're smart and skilled, so if you're not happy, then there are lots of other jobs. Do what you feel is right. You be you."

Ryan knew what felt right, but he also knew that Howard had been the one to put him up for the promotion. Howard had always been a great boss, encouraging, supportive, and understanding. Ryan hated the idea of letting him down.

"Ryan?" Howard interrupted Ryan's thoughts.

Ryan straightened in his chair and firmed his resolve. "Howard," said Ryan. "Thanks for standing up for me, I really appreciate it, but I can't take the promotion."

"What do you mean you can't take the promotion? Of course, you can. What's wrong, you need more time? I can probably get you a couple more weeks if Karisa needs more help."

Ryan shook his head. "My family needs me, Howard. Not just Karisa, but Joy and Michael too. And it wouldn't be fair to you and the firm. My head wouldn't be in the job."

"Ryan, I don't know when this opportunity will come around again. You are by far the best-qualified candidate for the job, everyone knows it."

"I understand. I just can't do that to my family right now. I hope this doesn't reflect badly on you."

Howard waved a dismissive hand before picking up his sandwich and taking another bite. "No need to worry about me, Ryan. I get it. There were probably a couple of times in my life where I could have made a similar decision and didn't. It took me a long time and a lot of therapy to realize that family is everything."

Ryan arrived home as Karisa finished putting dinner on the table. He kissed her cheek.

"Hi, hun. How was work?"

Ryan smiled. He felt like a large weight had been lifted from his chest. He felt like he could breathe for the first time in a long while. "It was good, really good. How are you feeling?"

"I feel fine, a little tired."

He kissed her again.

They had dinner, Ryan asking about the kids' day at school, then he did the dishes and helped with homework. When the kids were finally asleep, he joined Karisa in bed.

"I'm spent," he said.

Karisa put her book down and looked at him. "So, I got a call from the bank today and they asked if we wanted to refinance our home."

"Really? And do we?"

"Well, I was curious so I asked them to do some numbers to see what that would look like. John was right about the amortization and appreciation. We've been paying the mortgage for the last twelve years and the house is worth a lot more than when we bought it. We have nearly $100,000 in equity."

"What? That much?"

"Some of the books I read have given examples of people who have refinanced their homes and used the money to invest. I was talking with the agent, and we can refinance, lower our mortgage payments by $300 a month, and still cash out $50,000."

"I thought our goal had always been to pay off our house, so we wouldn't have a mortgage when we finally retired," said Ryan.

She nodded. "That was the goal." She put her head on his shoulder. "And it can still be the goal if you aren't comfortable with this because we're partners and we make decisions together. But maybe we need new goals for the house."

"Like what?"

"Well, getting a cash-out refinance is literally using 'other people's money' like John mentioned at the restaurant. Because it's a mortgage loan, the interest rate would be really low, and we could then use the cash-out to invest for higher interest returns. If we can reduce the interest rate on our house, lower the payments, and get cash out, then that would let us start investing in our future. I'd call that winning."

Ryan thought about it. "I mean, that makes sense."

"In the long run, the stock market would probably make us more than mortgage interest would cost us, but I've been thinking about what John and Jill said the other night."

"Investing in rental properties? I thought..."

"I know, but you've confined me to bed a lot the last couple of weeks, and I've been reading. I think we should do the refinance and ask John to connect us with one of his brokers. It's worth listening to an expert and seeing what our options are. If we don't like what he has to say, we can still invest in the stock market."

Ryan rubbed her shoulders as he thought. "Well, what do you think?" Karisa asked. "We're in a really great position now to get started. We thought my business might lose profits when we hired help, but it's still growing. We've made changes in the way we live, and that's helped us save so much more than we ever did before. Plus your promotion. Now's the time, right?"

"I turned down the promotion."

Karisa was quiet for a moment. "Are you sure that's what you want to do?"

He turned to look into her eyes and touched her cheek. "I haven't been this sure of something since I asked you to marry me."

CHAPTER EIGHTEEN

"Great to finally meet you," Aliya Williams said, smiling at Ryan and Karisa through the screen of a laptop which was perched on their dining room table.

Ryan had exchanged a couple of emails with her after John sent a virtual introduction, but this was their first meeting. Ryan had his Grow notebook, the fresh page already labeled, 'Real Estate Broker Meeting.'

He was excited about this video call. Beyond Karisa's business, they were finally starting to invest. He was nervous but strangely confident. They had done their homework, with John's help. They knew the questions to ask, and they even knew some of the answers now, too.

"Thanks a lot for calling, Aliya," said Karisa.

"No problem, I'm happy to give you guys the rundown. Oh, and thanks for filling out the questionnaire so thoroughly, it really helped me to understand you and your goals. What we're going to do today is work on creating a plan to reach those goals through income-producing real estate."

"How does your company work?" asked Karisa.

"Great question. We provide education and support for both new and experienced investors. We've been in business for almost twenty years. I have four investment counselors who work for me, and we all own investment properties as well. Today, I'm here to answer all your questions and talk about your way forward if you're ready."

"Sounds great," said Ryan.

"So, I saw in your comments that you have two kids and another child on the way. Congratulations! I also noticed that you want to focus on cash flow and future appreciation. That's great because the U.S. is the best place in the world to meet those goals, but it really depends on where you invest in the country."

"I'm thinking that California probably isn't the best?" asked Ryan

She laughed. "Not really. Currently, the midwest and the southeast are the best for that. You'll want to focus on metropolitan areas that are growing. We are constantly analyzing which markets in the U.S. are growing, and then we interview dozens of companies in those markets who have quality investment properties and experienced property management."

"What do you mean by 'metropolitan areas that are growing'?" asked Ryan.

"We like to say 'Where the people go, the money flows'. We look for markets with a diverse labor force, new companies starting up and hiring, old companies with solid reputations, and we look at which way the population is trending in those markets. That increases the odds of a good investment because there are more people looking to rent a home. With investing, selecting the right market is even more important than selecting the right property."

Ryan took notes.

"How do you find these brokers and property teams around the country?" asked Karisa.

"Another good question. The truth is that when I started out, I used to do all the legwork myself, flying all over the country to check out markets, talk with property managers and hunt down income properties for sale. Now, I'm fortunate enough to have good employees who analyze the different markets in the U.S. in order to find those that have the key metrics for investing, talk to property brokers nationwide, walk through properties to check their condition, analyze the numbers, and then do background checks to make sure everything is legit. We have a full set of written standards and a complete process for analyzing markets, brokers, property teams, and properties before we refer our investors to them."

"Wow, that sounds like a lot of work. Do you mind if I ask how you get reimbursed for all your time and information?" Ryan asked.

"Of course, that's a fair question. Like any real estate brokerage, we receive a referral fee when a client purchases a property through a broker that we recommended."

"So, when we purchase the property the other broker pays you?"

"Yes, but it doesn't end up costing you any more because the fee is paid as a percentage of the normal broker commission, which is paid by the person who sold the property."

"Ah, I understand."

"These real estate referrals happen all the time, especially when a real estate broker isn't able to service their client in the purchase of property in a particular geographic area. It's a true win-win-win. The person selling the property finds a buyer, the broker listing the property is compensated by the seller, we are compensated by that broker for helping them find a buyer, and the buyer is happy because they were able to locate a property they couldn't have found on their own."

"That makes sense."

"So, tell me more about your goals with investing. What is your *why*?"

"Well," Karisa began, "to be fully transparent, we're just on a fact-finding mission right now to determine if this is the right way forward for us. Also, I just want you to know that I'm coming to this meeting with an open mind, but I was really opposed to real estate investing for a while."

"Why is that?"

"It's really complicated, and there is a lot of contradictory information out there. And then there is the cost—it's a lot of money to put in one place."

"I completely understand. It's smart to want to understand what you're investing in. And I'm here to clarify anything you don't understand, so ask me all the questions you want. If you don't mind my asking, what changed your mind?"

"Well, Jill and John, mostly. Seeing the way they live—not just their material wealth, but the time they have to spend with one another—it made me realize that there was a different way to live life."

Ryan reached out and grabbed Karisa's hand. "For so long, we were sure that if I just worked harder, worked more hours, then we'd finally make enough money to live our dreams. But Karisa is right, seeing John and Jill really changed things for us, especially seeing how strong their relationship is. We want that. I want that—time with my kids, my wife—but we still want material things too. I think we're both hoping that if we can generate cash flow with rental properties, it will help us with both." What he had told Howard was true, his priorities were different than six months ago, and they didn't revolve around climbing the corporate ladder unless that ascent also included spending more time with his family.

Karisa nodded her agreement. "Neither of us is opposed to hard work—in fact, I have a growing business that I really enjoy—but we don't want work to consume our lives either. It felt like we had to pick between having a tightly-knit family or having money. Now we know we don't have to choose, and we're taking steps toward a future with both."

Her words resonated with Ryan. He knew he had to make a salary to support his family, and he accepted that. But Karisa was right; his skills were in high demand. He had the experience and training. His current job wasn't his only option. Karisa's home business was working pretty well, and with the savings they'd made lately, they could definitely float for a few months while he found something that made sense for his family. Something that would make both Karisa and him happy. Coupled with their new real estate investing plans, he was starting to picture a very different life for himself and his family.

"Alright guys, I totally understand where you're coming from. I think everyone in my office and most of my clients have been there at one time or another. Given how much you're prepared to invest, I suggest you start out small and buy one single-family investment property. I think Texas or Florida are some good places to start with the best chance of cash flow and appreciation from day one. I'm going to put you in contact with three brokers located in those states. They have experienced and high-quality property managers who have proven to be on top of things in the past."

Ryan wrote down the states and circled the names. Then wrote 'PM cost???'.

"How much do property managers charge, and won't that affect our overall cash flow?" asked Karisa, glancing at the notebook.

"Yes and no. Most property managers charge around eight to ten percent, but it's totally worth it and absolutely necessary. They find quality tenants for your properties, oversee the maintenance, handle all the leases and collections, and they send you monthly financial statements so you can track your property's performance. Property management on your own can be very challenging, especially from across the country, so having an expert who knows the market and is close to your property is fully worth every cent in my opinion. You'll never have to deal with tenants, toilets, or trash. This allows you to invest in markets that aren't near you and concentrate most of your efforts on looking for more good investment properties."

"Aliya, can you go over the numbers for us. I'm not a hundred percent clear on that yet," said Karisa.

"Obviously, the numbers are the most important part of the equation, because if you aren't earning cash flow from day one, you need to find another property. All of this is found in what we call the Pro forma, which is basically a combined and simplified Income Statement and Cash Flow Statement specifically made for your property and your situation. These generally include your rental income minus management fees, operating expenses, taxes, and other factors that affect your cash flow."

Ryan covered Karisa's hand with his. "What do you think, babe?"

Karisa nodded slowly. "Let's look at some of these properties."

"What's our next step, Aliya?" asked Ryan.

"Well, I'll send you the contact information for those three brokers, and I'll let them know you will be reaching out to them. You can either fly out to visit their markets and see their available properties in person, or you can simply review the information they send you about their available properties, look at the photos of the properties, and probably a video walk-through of the properties. Of course, they will also send you a pro forma on each property so you can review and compare the numbers with the other options you have from other brokers and property teams."

"Sounds great!" said Ryan.

"One more thing," said Aliya. "Whatever approach you take, always make sure to do your own due diligence, get an inspection and an appraisal from a third party professional before you buy anything. The brokers I refer you to will support that and will never tell you to buy a property without an inspection or an appraisal. It's what we demand to keep our investors safe and secure."

"Thanks for the advice, we appreciate it," said Ryan.

"And while you're waiting to contact the brokers, you might want to pre-qualify for a loan if you haven't already."

"How do I do that?" asked Ryan.

"I'll send you some phone numbers for several loan brokers who specialize in investor loans. It's helpful to find out how much of a loan you can get before shopping for an income property. You'll have to put down about twenty to twenty-five percent and then finance the rest. Of course, when you purchase the right property, the monthly rental payments will more than cover the costs of the loan, the property taxes, the management fees, and even the repairs in the future. By getting pre-qualified for a loan, you'll be able to take action right away when a broker shows you a property that you want to purchase."

Ryan wrote in his notebook. "We'll get on that tomorrow, and we'll send emails to the brokers as soon as we get the contact info from you."

"If you have any other questions, please feel free to reach out to me. I'm really excited for you two. Buying your first investment property is usually the most challenging step for most new investors, but once you do it, you'll notice a big shift in the way you see investing and how quickly you will learn and feel even more comfortable with real estate investing. I remember how scared and excited I was to buy my first rental property, but now I own dozens of properties all over the country, and they have truly brought me to a place of financial freedom. I love seeing others follow the path, and I feel it's my purpose to help people gain peace of mind and create more freedom in their lives."

They said their goodbyes and hung up with Aliya, then sat in silence with their own thoughts.

"So," Karisa said after a while, "We're going to do this."

"I think so."

"But no rush, we take it slow and make deliberate choices together."

"No stress." He tried to hold her hand, but she pulled away and cradled his face between her palms.

"No stress," she said and kissed him.

CHAPTER NINETEEN

"You're looking really fit, Ryan," said John.

The early morning sun shone down as they continued their mostly uphill hike. They were an hour away from Tattoo Point, and Ryan's shirt was soaked with sweat, but he hadn't lagged behind, and that made him happy. That, and the beautiful morning.

"Thanks for noticing, but I have to give credit to your gym's adventure routines, they're no joke. You really have some good people working for you there." Ryan took a slug of water from his CamelBak, sighing in relief as the cool liquid hit his parched throat.

"I'm really grateful for those good people. When you're running your own business, finding the right people is key to your success. That's one of the most important lessons I want you to remember."

"How about I file that away in my Grow book with all the other great stuff I've learned from you."

They paused at a lookout point. Ryan gazed out over a canyon at a majestic pair of falcons soaring above a group of rock climbers.

"Is that the same climbing area we saw on our bike ride?"

"Yes, it is. That's Echo Cliff, just from a different angle."

"Do all rock-climbing locations have interesting names?"

John laughed. "Usually interesting or inspiring. My favorite is called 'A Steep Climb Named Desire'."

Ryan laughed too, then got serious as he watched the climbers. "I think I'm ready to try some real rocks when you have time."

"Really? Fantastic! I'll set it up. You're really going to love it."

They began moving down the path again.

"So, I heard you spoke with Aliya. Did you guys decide on a property?"

Ryan nodded at John's back as he stepped around a small outcropping of rock. "She was great, thanks so much for connecting us. Karisa and I reached out to the brokers she suggested and we decided on a property in Florida, in the Orlando area." Ryan smiled warmly at the memory. "Joy overheard us talking about Orlando and immediately began trying to convince us to plan a trip."

"That's a good market," said John.

"Yeah, we built up a decent amount of savings thanks to our frugal living and refinanced our house for the down payment. So we still have enough savings to make sure we're comfortable with everything."

"Smart, Ryan. And when you inspect your property there, you can write off the trip on your taxes. So, it might be worth your while to go to Disney with the kids."

"Good to know, Joy will be happy to hear that."

John laughed. "I'm sure she will. Also, I like how you're easing into this and learning the different phases."

"Planting phase."

"Exactly. The planting phase. Also, it sounds like you are prepared for the unexpected. No need to stress and overextend yourselves. You're going to see how this will make you wealthy in so many ways, beyond the financial. I know some people who are so poor, all they have is money. They are poor in life, or they make a lot of money but work so much they don't have time to enjoy life. The truly wealthy people that I know have so much more than money. They have freedom, health, and vitality. They have peace of mind. And they have fulfillment."

"Real wealth," said Ryan.

"Ah, you remember! Well, if you understand real wealth, then you might be on the verge of graduating from my humble university. You've already learned a lot of the ways that wealthy people think and act differently than most other people."

The trail narrowed and John took the lead, ducking between two large boulders that leaned against each other to make a short tunnel. A chipmunk perched on top chattered at Ryan as he approached, clutching an acorn to its chest protectively.

Ryan chuckled softly before following. "What ways?"

"Most importantly, you've learned the value of time. Wealthy people invest their money into freeing up their time. Most people don't seem to value the time they have, but you've definitely learned its importance, haven't you?"

"I'm a little slow, but I'm figuring it out."

"Wealthy people want time to spend with family, friends and to make the world a better place, so they focus on building wealth in order to actually buy back their time. Most people today buy things and then spend a lot of their time working to pay for them. They trade time for money in order to accumulate more things that don't build wealth, thus actually decreasing their wealth."

"So, wealthy people value their time. Got it. What else?"

They came to a fork, and John led them down the route back to Tattoo Point.

"Well, wealthy people are constantly educating themselves about money and investing. Most people seem to escape into entertainment, which is fine as long as it doesn't take over their life and prevent them from learning and growing."

"Karisa and I are knee-deep in wealth education at this point."

"Excellent. Also, and this goes back to managing time, most people only think about working for money. Paying their bills is all they worry about, and they're stuck in a vicious cycle of continually having to work for the money they'll never have enough of because they're not putting that money to work for them. Wealthy people multiply their money by growing it through investments. Real financial independence means never having to worry about how the bills are going to be paid."

Ryan nodded. "I remember being stuck there."

"Yeah, but you're buying your first rental property, so you are on your way toward financial independence."

"Karisa and I have been doing the numbers. Even without my promotion, between her business, the Airbnb income, and the rental property, we should be able to invest in another property by the end of the year. And I've been thinking about freelancing online for some extra cash."

John smiled. "The saving to invest cycle becomes a little addicting once you see your future, doesn't it?"

"It's like we finally have a destination."

A cool breeze blew through the trees as they started climbing up toward Tattoo Point, Ryan side by side with John.

"Where's that destination for you guys?" John asked.

"Living life on our own terms."

They climbed the last steps to the painted platform, and John turned to Ryan.

"I can see the changes you've made over the last six months. Do you feel different?"

Ryan sat down on the edge that they had rappelled down months ago, looking over the valley and listening to the waterfall below. "I do. I feel like my eyes have been opened."

"Then there's one more thing I want to tell you about wealthy people, and this is just something to consider as Karisa and you continue on your journey. Wealthy people have much more than just a retirement plan. They plan to leave wealth for their heirs and charitable causes for generations to come. They have a strong desire to give back and contribute to the world, to make a difference, and ultimately to create a legacy."

Ryan sipped some more water from his CamelBak. *What will be my legacy?* he thought.

CHAPTER TWENTY

"I want to take this opportunity to congratulate Clint, who has been promoted to be our new Junior Manager of Coders," said Patterson, glaring at Ryan as he spoke. "Clint has displayed the attitude and expertise CaptivSoft expects in its managers. We are confident that he will be an excellent mentor and leader for years to come."

The Office had assembled in the front foyer by the elevators as Patterson gave his speech. Ryan clapped with everyone else. *Good for Clint*, thought Ryan. *A good choice*. Clint came to the company a few years after Ryan, but he was a good coder and had great organizational skills.

Everyone stood in line to congratulate the new junior manager.

"Great job, Clint," Ryan told him.

"I'm as surprised as you are, Ryan, this is crazy. They approached me last week."

"You deserve it, you're going to do great."

"I'll talk to Howard and Patterson. I mean, you basically mentored me when I got here."

"Really, buddy, don't worry about it. They picked the right guy." Ryan made room for the next well-wisher. As the crowd died down, Ryan joined the flow of people returning to their desks.

Patterson was waiting at Ryan's workstation. "In my office, now," he growled as he turned away.

Ryan followed, wondering what this was about.

Patterson shut the door, then went to stand behind his desk. "Who do you think you are?"

"Excuse me, sir? What are we talking about?"

Patterson pointed at Ryan. "You knew we were grooming you for that junior management job. And you had the audacity to decline the position?"

"Look, sir, I meant no disrespect…"

"I just don't understand you, Brooks. You know that because you turned this position down, you'll never get offered another one, right? If nothing else, I'll make sure of that."

Ryan paused. "I wasn't aware of that, but thanks for explaining it to me." Ryan stood and turned to leave.

"Where are you going? I'm not finished talking to you."

Ryan turned at the door and looked Patterson in the eye. His mind raced. He felt pressure building up in his chest. Hope was coming. He needed this job for his family. He...

Ryan took a deep breath.

"Sit down," ordered Patterson.

He didn't need this job. That was his Gremlin talking. His family needed him. Turning down that promotion was the best decision he had made at the company in a long time. Until now.

"Thanks for the talk, Dave. You really cleared some things up for me."

"Oh yeah, what's that?"

"That I'm not happy working here, so I quit."

"Oh come on now, don't be ridiculous."

"I'll clear out my desk today." Ryan turned again.

Patterson laughed out loud. "Don't say things you aren't ready to do."

Ryan opened the door.

"Hey, Ryan," Patterson called in a raised voice, so everyone in the surrounding cubicles could hear. "Tell me really, why did you turn down the promotion? Didn't think you could hack it?"

Ryan stopped just outside the door and paused. "You really want to know why?"

"Yeah, tell me."

"I didn't want to end up like you."

———————

The sound of whistles blowing and kids shouting reached Ryan's ears as he exited his car at the soccer field. He spotted Karisa in the bleachers, intently watching the game with Joy at her side. She jumped to her feet as Michael's team scored a goal.

Ryan took a deep breath and blew it out. This wasn't the day he had anticipated, that was for sure. He had been thinking about leaving the company at some point, but not today. He felt different though. Karisa was right. There were other opportunities out there if he wanted them, just as good or maybe even better.

He walked toward the beautiful woman he had asked to marry thirteen years ago, who he had promised to be with for better or worse. This felt better.

"Hey, babe," he said, sitting beside her.

"Oh jeez, you scared me," she said, then hugged him tightly. "They just scored."

"I saw."

"To what do we owe this unexpected appearance," she asked with a smile. "It's been a while since you made a game. Is this the new 'present' Ryan?"

He smiled too. "It is for the near future. I just quit my job."

Her surprised face, mouth slightly open, was priceless. He kissed her.

"I've decided to freelance for a bit. It'll be good. I'll help with your business and around the house during these last few months before the baby's born."

"Oh, hun. Are you alright?"

"Yeah, I'm good." He put his arm around her. "Let's enjoy the game."

"Are you sure?"

"I'm sure. Actually, I'm more than sure. I'm at peace about it."

Ryan squeezed her and watched his son successfully defend the goal. Joy moved around her mom to sit on his other side, and he put his other arm around her.

He felt a weight lift from him. He felt happy.

This is what I want for my life, he thought. *My family is my priority.* He kissed the top of Joy's head. *I'll find a way to have it all. If I have to, I'll make my own way.*

CHAPTER
TWENTY-ONE

Ryan stood in line at the post office with a cart of twenty boxed moss art projects. *This seems a little antiquated*, he thought. *Drones drop things off on doorsteps for Amazon now, I bet there's some kind of pickup service for this kind of thing.* He saw some flyers about home pickup and pocketed them.

Karisa had been making the postal runs a couple of times a week for the last year, and now their hired help was doing it for her, which was fine, but there had to be another way. At CaptivSoft, Ryan had always felt he couldn't understand the problems completely until he did the work, so he had insisted Karisa walk him through each stage of her business to see if he had any ideas for process improvement.

He hadn't applied for any contract jobs yet. Karisa had convinced him to take a break, help out with the business, spend some time with the kids, and just relax. Reluctantly, he had agreed, but after three weeks, he felt great, focused, and, to be honest, a little restless. He had entered the annual neighborhood BBQ competition, something he'd always wanted to do but had previously never had the spare time to participate. After he'd read the rules, he'd reached out to the sponsors and volunteered to make a downloadable app to help with public voting. While there were judges, Ryan suggested having a people's choice award might be of interest. He just needed something to occupy his mind, and since he was doing it for free, they agreed. It only took him a day, and they were really happy with the results.

He reached the front of the line, set the boxes on the counter and paid the bill.

A sign on the desk advertised USPS Mobile—even the post office had an app.

Maybe what he had said to Karisa at the soccer game was the way to go. Maybe freelancing could bring in some extra cash. His health insurance with CaptivSoft ran out at the end of the month, so if he didn't get a job that included insurance, he'd have to start paying out of pocket. It was time to do some research on freelance jobs and some cost analysis on losing the benefits of a company like CaptivSoft.

———————

"What are you doing, hun?" asked Karisa.

Ryan swiveled around and she giggled as he brought her into his lap. "Lots of different things."

Ryan had spent the last four hours in his office, researching and taking notes in his Grow notebook. Grabbing it off the table, he opened it in her lap so she could see.

"Like what?"

He flipped through some pages. "Where to start?" Flipped a couple more. "I have some ideas about your business that I want to talk about with you which I think will make things go smoother, but let's do that later. Right now, I want to talk about this." He stopped on a page with a bunch of numbers.

"What am I looking at?"

"It's basically our current cash flow."

"Oh no, are we in trouble?"

"No, no. That's the point. I think we're doing really well. Between what your business is making, our Airbnb, and the initial rental income we're receiving, we're at about seventy-five percent what I was making before I quit. And with the big cuts we made in our expenses, we actually bank more money at the end of every month. However, if I don't get a job that provides medical and dental coverage, we're going to have to start paying for that. I also researched some self-employed health insurance plans, and even after paying for that, we still break a bit more than even."

"Why are you telling me all this? Don't you want to go back to work?"

"Well, I was thinking of giving freelancing a try. There are a bunch of websites where I can advertise my skills and get people to hire me. I just want to make sure you're on board."

Karisa was quiet. Ryan felt her breathing. "What happens if freelancing doesn't work? I'm a little concerned about the healthcare, especially with the baby coming."

"I know, me too. That's why I picked the best coverage I could find for what we need, comparable, to my CaptivSoft coverage. The numbers work. Plus, your business keeps growing."

"But what if it stops growing, or we have some low earning months?"

Ryan stroked her head. "Here's what I'm thinking, and you have full veto rights. Let me try freelancing for three months, then we'll look at where we're at. We'll re-evaluate our financial situation together every week, and if we decide it's not working, or we start dipping into our savings too much, then I'll start hunting for a full-time job. If after three months, I've made no headway with finding any freelance work, then I'll look for a full-time job. But if after three months I'm earning at least $3,000 dollars a month, then we'll reassess and make a new plan of action. What do you think?"

She was quiet again.

"Babe?" he asked.

She sighed. "Can we make it two months? I just want to be sure we have insurance for when the baby arrives."

He squeezed her. "Two months it is."

Ryan's cell rang, and Karisa pushed herself off so he could grab it from the desk.

"Hello?"

"Hello, my name is Arthur Cochrane," came the voice on the other end. "I'm trying to reach Ryan Brooks."

"This is Ryan. How can I help you?"

"I was one of the judges at the BBQ cookoff last weekend and was told that you were the brain behind the people's choice app. Is that your original design?"

Damn, Ryan thought. *I knew it was too easy. My app is probably too similar to something already out there.*

"I'd like to reassure you that everything in that app is my own, but if you need me to take it down, I can do that. No problem."

"No, no. Don't take it down. I'm the secretary for the state BBQ board next month, and I was wondering if your app could handle larger audiences."

"Well, it's just a basic app. It shouldn't be a problem, but I can tweak it to make it smoother if necessary." Ryan sighed. *No good deed goes unpunished. You do something simple for free and everyone wants a piece of the action.*

"Great. Do you think you could stop by my office sometime this week? I'll put you in touch with my assistant. I'll get some planners together and we can discuss a few improvements."

"Sure, I guess I could do that."

"And send your rates over to my assistant when you get a chance."

"My rates?"

"Yeah, so we can get your contract together. We'll need a W-9 filled out too. We'll probably be able to integrate this into a few other things we're working on, so we'll just add you to our contracting staff. Work it out with my assistant when she calls. See you then."

"Thanks. Bye."

The line went dead. Ryan stared at the phone.

"Who was that?" asked Karisa.

Ryan looked at her and smiled. "That was the future calling."

CHAPTER
TWENTY-TWO

"Okay, Ryan, you got this. Look for a foothold."

Ryan's forearms burned, and his sweat-drenched shirt clung to his body as the sun beat down on his back and neck. He'd been building up to this over the last five years, working hard at John's gym and doing some occasional rock climbing excursions, but this was the most difficult by far. He hooked the fingers of his right hand in a small crevice and reached behind for some chalk with his left. Then he shook his left arm a few times and continued his climb. As he slowly moved his right foot up, he felt the small protrusion through his climbing shoe. He knew it would support him. He looked up, identified his next hand hold, and slowly, but steadily, progressed up the rockface to John, who pulled rope up on belay.

Five minutes later, Ryan sat at the top next to John, drinking cool water and looking out over the canyon below. The sun began to set, painting the rock walls in a stunning array of pinks, oranges, and yellows.

"So this is what it looks like from up here," said Ryan.

John laughed. "You climbed that well, you should be proud. Sunset Bouldervard is a tough route. A 5.11 is advanced climbing by anyone's standards."

They were quiet for a bit, with only the rustling of the wind and chattering of squirrels filling the space around them. Ryan was lost in his thoughts about how much his life had changed since he had first seen climbers on this rock while hiking with John five years ago.

John stood and stretched. "We better start heading down or it will be dark when we hit the trail."

Ryan helped him coil the rope, and they started hiking down the trail.

"Did you get moved in okay?" asked John.

Ryan nodded. "Everything moved and most of the boxes unpacked. The house looks great, you and Jill need to come over."

CHAPTER TWENTY-TWO

"Say when."

"Let me check with Karisa, but soon."

"Great. And we haven't seen Hope in almost six months."

"You won't even recognize her, she's grown so much."

It was getting dark when they reached the parking lot and put the equipment into John's truck.

"I got something for you," said John, reaching into the cab. He handed Ryan a rectangular package wrapped in brown paper. "Housewarming gift."

"You didn't have to do this," said Ryan.

"Open it."

Ryan tore the paper to reveal a framed photo of himself rappelling down Tattoo Point, taken from above. "I didn't know you took a photo." Ryan studied it, the waterfall shooting out below his feet as he concentrated on the rockface. He looked back at John, barely able to see his eyes glint in the last of the sun's rays. "Thanks, John."

"You're welcome. I'm glad you like it."

Ryan shook his head. "Not just for this. I don't know if we would have gotten here without all your advice and…"

"You don't owe me anything. You and Karisa made your own way."

"Still, I just don't know how to thank you for everything you've done for my family."

John came forward, grabbed his shoulders and smiled. "Seeing you happy and successful is reward enough for me. I wouldn't be where I am without the mentors in my life. Whatever you think I did to help you, I'm just paying it forward."

———————

Ryan walked into the new house with John's gift under his arm. He still thought of it that way. The new house. *How long before I consider this my home?* he thought.

In the living room, he saw that Karisa had been unpacking. Half-empty boxes were strewn about the room. Some pictures and knick-knacks had found homes on the shelves. Above the mantle was the family portrait they had made last year. Ryan walked out the sliding back door and followed a stone path to a large barn-like structure. Lights streamed out from the windows and door.

Inside, his wife was organizing chaos. Her four employees set up tables and unpacked more boxes while she directed from the center. A workshop for her ever-growing business had been a must when they had talked with the architect. He smiled while watching her work. He thought about how much he appreciated the connection they shared. Best friends, partners, and lovers.

Returning to the house, he stopped at each of the kid's rooms. Michael was reading a magazine with his headphones on but turned off the music when he entered.

"Don't you need to get some rest? I want to watch you play in your soccer game tomorrow, not take a nap on the sidelines."

"Yeah. Five more minutes."

Ryan nodded, then moved on to Joy's room. She was already asleep but had kicked off her blankets, and he gently tucked her back in and kissed her cheek before heading down the hall to Hope's room

When he opened the door, he found the bed empty. Panic gripping him, he turned and nearly fled from the room as his mind scrambled for what to do next. Only the sight of his own bedroom door, pushed slightly ajar, gave him pause. Pushing it open fully, he spotted the familiar little head peeking out from the top of the covers right in the middle of his and Karisa's bed.

His heart warmed as he smiled in relief. This was his life.

He went back downstairs to his office. Behind his desk were photos of the twelve properties they had managed to acquire over the last five years. Almost $5,000 a month in monthly cash flow. A portfolio valued at over $2,000,000. Sometimes it just blew his mind. He never would have thought they could have this.

He sat down, put the framed photo on the desk, and smiled.

This was his home.

WHAT'S NEXT

A variety of free resources can be found at:
realwealth.com/grow

On that page you will find:

RYAN'S GROW NOTEBOOK

A downloadable version of Ryan's notebook with his notes and big ideas from mentoring with John, including his favorite lessons, thoughts, ideas, and action items.

THE LIFE WHEEL

Complete your own Life Wheel to clarify how you are feeling about ten major areas of your life. It's helpful to fill out a Life Wheel every 3–6 months to reflect on what is working and what might need your attention.

THE REALWEALTH ASSESSMENT™

How would you rate your level of *real* wealth? Do you have the money and freedom to live life on your own terms? Are you fulfilled? How is your well-being? Where are you now, and where would you like to be? The RealWealth Assessment™ helps you measure, manage, and track your progress over time in those areas of life that bring you *real* wealth and fulfillment. This is another tool that is helpful to complete every 3–6 months.

FUTURE SELF (AUDIO)

Sit back and listen to the full future-self visualization that John took Ryan through. You'll meet your future self — your wise, inner mentor who will help answer your most important questions. You'll be able to envision what your future will look like if everything turns out just right.

INVESTMENT COUNSELORS & PROPERTIES

Since 2003, the RealWealth network has helped members build financial freedom by simplifying the process of real-estate investing. Membership is free and will give you access to hundreds of educational videos, articles, webinars, and access to investment properties nationwide.

RealWealth investment counselors will help you get the information you need to make an informed decision. They connect you with property teams nationwide with proven track records so that you can choose your investments. Your investment counselor is there to coach you as needed, and you can also gain access to investing in larger commercial projects, syndications, and funds.

ACKNOWLEDGMENTS

As I write these acknowledgments, I'm presented with the challenge of keeping this section from doubling the size of this book. For all of you who have been with me on this journey, whom I have not thanked in the following paragraphs, please know that I appreciate you more than you can imagine.

First and foremost, I want to thank my wife, Kathy Fettke, for being such an amazing human, wife, friend, lover, co-parent, and business partner. I am deeply grateful for our 25+ years of love, fun, adventure, passion, support, and belief.

Karina Vitale, thank you for all the love you bring to my life. I'm extra grateful to you and Pat for creating Leo. He's such an awesome grandson and has added so much laughter and love to our lives.

Krista Fettke, you are still my little "clone" and there's nothing you can do to change that. Thank you for being such a wise, loving soul and for always being a fun rock climbing partner...ever since you were just a toddler.

To my mom, Mari Fettke: thank you for how well you handled me as a "hyperkinetic" kid and for always holding the belief that someday I'd channel that energy toward something positive. Words can not express how much I appreciate and love you.

Massive thanks to you, Randy Surles, for helping me create a captivating, inspiring and powerful story. And thank you for bringing the talented Laura Graves into the process. The two of you were a joy to work with.

Thanks to Robert Kiyosaki for helping millions of people improve their financial intelligence and for the thoughtful foreword for this book.

A big thank you to Ken McElroy for being a great friend, a total giver, and an overall cool dude. I have tons of respect and admiration for you and Danille.

Thank you, to Mona Gambetta, for helping me navigate the publishing process and for your valuable feedback and constant encouragement.

I am grateful for my personal coach, Kenji Oshima, for asking me powerful questions and for helping me better understand how to honor what I value most. You've helped me become a better human being. And thanks for constantly asking me over the years, "So when are you going to write your next book?" Well, here it is!

Thank you to the beta readers of my manuscript: Tonya Allen, Boomer Angove, Mike Ayala, Donna Behrens, Dusty Breeding, Kristine Carlson, Leah Collich, Jeffrey Conway, Kathy Fettke, Krista Fettke, Mari Fettke, Jon Gordon, Pat Henggeler, Aristotle Kumpis, Brad LeCraw, Maggie McKinnie, Julian Paige, Kelley Pecoraro, Mike Robbins, Amy Searcy, Joe Torre, Brandon Turner, and Tarl Yarber. Your valuable feedback helped improve the story and the lessons shared.

A big thank you to the thousands of members of RealWealth for being part of our network and for sharing your stories, many of which have been woven into the story in this book. Your desire to learn, grow, invest, and live life on your own terms has helped not only you and your family, but also anyone who reads this book.

And of course, to our whole team at RealWealth for all you have done to help us live our purpose and achieve our mission. That includes every employee, contractor, and all of the amazing property teams around the country who take such good care of RealWealth investors. The only thing more important than a great idea is the team that can see it through!

And finally, thank you for reading this book. You obviously care about learning and growing. I wish you the best on your journey of financial freedom and living a fun, fulfilling life.

ABOUT THE AUTHOR

Rich Fettke is a licensed real estate broker, active investor, and Co-Founder of RealWealth®, a real estate investment group that helps its 60,000+ members improve their financial intelligence, secure passive income, and obtain financial freedom. He's also the author of *Extreme Success* (Simon & Schuster, 2002) and the audio program, *Momentum*. A pioneer in the field of business and personal coaching, Rich is a former vice president of the International Coach Federation (ICF) and holds one of the ICF's first Master Certified Coach credentials. Rich's work has been featured on TV, radio, and in print including *USA Today*, *Entrepreneur Magazine*, and *The Wall Street Journal*. A passionate adventure athlete, Rich lives in Malibu, California, with his wife Kathy, where they invest, work, and play together. He hopes to someday be as wise as the mentor in this story.